THE VOYA

The Voyage of the *Komagata Maru*

The Sikh Challenge to Canada's Colour Bar

HUGH JOHNSTON

UBC PRESS / VANCOUVER

Printed in Canada

ISBN 0-7748-0340-1

Canadian Cataloguing in Publication Data

Johnston, H.J.M. (Hugh J.M.), 1939-
    The voyage of the Komagata Maru

    Includes bibliographical references and index.
    ISBN 0-7748-0340-1

    1. Komagata Maru Incident, 1914.* 2 Sikhs –
Canada – History. 3. East Indians – Canada –
History. 4. Aliens – Canada – History.
I. Title.
JV7285.S54J64 1989   325′.254′0971   C89-091374-9

UBC Press
University of British Columbia
6344 Memorial Road
Vancouver, BC V6T 1Z2
(604) 822-3259
Fax: (604) 822-6083

This book has been published with the help of a grant from the Canada
Council.

To the memory of
KARTAR SINGH
who came to Canada nonetheless

Besides, the visions of men are widened by travel and
contact with citizens of a free country will infuse a spirit
of independence and foster yearning for freedom in the
minds of the emasculated subjects of alien rule.

Gurdit Singh
Voyage of Komagatamaru

CONTENTS

PLATES

(between pages 54 and 55)

The passengers dressed to go ashore, 23 May 1914—Gurdit Singh, fore
ground left, with his son, Balwant, and, to his left, Daljit Singh.

Gurdit Singh with binoculars.

H.H. Stevens, centre, meets the press on board the tug *Sea Lion*, with Mal
colm Reid standing third from left, and Hopkinson on extreme right.

Scene in Vancouver Harbour, 21 July 1914. HMCS *Rainbow* called to aid i
deporting passengers on board *Komagata Maru*.

ACKNOWLEDGEMENTS

A grant from the President's Research Fund, Simon Fraser University, helped speed the research for this book. My thanks to S. K. Mathur and to Miss Kanwal Arora for their extensive translations from Hindi and Gurmukhi; to Mark Hopkins, W. B. Yeo, and Bryan Corbett, of the Public Archives Canada; to George Brandak, Special Collections, University of British Columbia; and to Bill McKee, Assistant Archivist, and Lynn Ogden, former Archivist, City Archives, Vancouver, for guidance to archival materials; to Arun Coomer Bose, Professor of History, University of Jammu, S. S. Saxena and T. R. Sareen, of the National Archives of India, Dharma Vir, Nehru Memorial Museum and Library, New Delhi, A. B. Roy, Assistant Librarian, National Library, Calcutta, and to Andrew S. Cook, Miss U. Tripathi, A. Griffin, and T. Thomas, of the India Office Library, for ready replies to my inquiries; to Mrs Pat Leger, Government Documents Librarian, S.F.U., for many letters and searches; the Vancouver Public Library for permission to reproduce the photographs; to Mrs Louise E. Post, Tom Warren, and fellow genealogists for their freely offered time in pursuit of Hopkinson's birth records; to Paul Brar and to G. S. Sangra for their generous help; to my colleagues, especially Douglas Cole, Robin Fisher, and George Cook, for encouragement in the early stages of research and writing; to Barry Gough for suggesting the subject; to Darrell Zarn and to David Barnhill for technical advice; to Mrs Jane Deal for a clean manuscript; to Brian for his interest and recruitment of his friend; and to Patricia for long days in the archives besides everything else.

I

EXCLUSION

In the first decade of this century, as a network of secret revolutionary societies spread from the Panjab and Bengal to Indian communities overseas, an intelligence organization grew apace. This organization depended on a small number of dedicated secret service officers, not the least of whom was William Charles Hopkinson, a man long since remembered in the Indian community in Vancouver.

Hopkinson was born in Delhi in 1880, his father then a sergeant instructor of volunteers at Allahabad, and he grew up in northern India speaking the local languages. In 1903 or 1904, he became an inspector of police in Calcutta and he remained there until sometime in 1907 or early 1908 when he came to Vancouver.[1] In February 1909, he was hired by the Canadian government as an immigration inspector and interpreter. But he never stopped working for the Indian police.

In intelligence matters, Hopkinson reported to the Deputy Minister of the Interior in Ottawa and to J. A. Wallinger, Agent of the Government of India, in London. He had access to criminal intelligence material from India that none of his Canadian superiors were supposed to see, and his connections were such that, in the United States, the American Commissioner-General of Immigration smoothed the path for his inquiries. He drew an annual salary from the Canadian government, a stipend and expenses from the India Office, and a retainer from the American immigration service. All this had the approval of his superiors in the Department of the Interior. It was his job to keep tabs on Indians, to know their movements and activities, and the more contacts he had, the better he could do it.[2]

There was no one else like him in the immigration service, no inspector with special language skills who was so exclusively con-

cerned with a single ethnic group. Not even the Chinese and the
Japanese merited such attention. Of course, Hopkinson was not
there to help the Indians, but to control them. The relationship
was adversary. 'Mr. Hopkinson commands the Pacific coast for
the Hindus', they complained, and the charge was not so far-
fetched.

Most of them were Panjabi Sikhs: rural people who had mortgaged their land at ten and twelve per cent interest to raise the
fare to Vancouver—$65 would be enough—in the expectation of
wages ten and fifteen times as high as anything they could hope
to earn in India. In lumber yards and saw mills in the vicinity of
Vancouver and Victoria they could make $1.50 or $2.00[3] a day,
and living frugally, three and four to a room, on a sparse but
adequate diet, they saved most of what they earned. What they
saved was never banked, but invested in real estate and in this way
some had accumulated $3,000, $4,000, and $5,000 since arriving
in Canada.[4] The objective was always to go back to their villages
where even $200 would be a fortune, and, while most were single,
there were a good number with wives in India.

The first of these Sikhs had come to Canada in 1904, encouraged
by the Hong Kong agents of the Canadian Pacific Railway
(C.P.R.), who were seeking to replace steerage traffic lost after
the Canadian government had raised the head tax on Chinese
immigrants.[5] Five Sikhs, bearded, turbaned, and wearing light
cotton European-style clothing, had arrived on the *Empress of
India* in March 1904; ten came on the *Empress of Japan* in May
and each succeeding month brought two or three more. It was
a strange country; few of the Sikhs could read, write, or even
speak English, and so, while there was work for them, especially
in the absence of continued Chinese immigration, it took them
some time to find it. Some were taken on by saw mills and a
cement factory; others by contractors who employed them on
the roads or in cutting wood and clearing land, and in a few
months they began sending home postal orders of $15, $20, and
$50.

Malaya and Hong Kong had long offered Sikhs employment
as policemen, watchmen, and caretakers—in preference to local
Chinese—and from these colonies some Sikhs had found their
way to Thailand, Sumatra, Shanghai, and Manila. North America
was a new discovery. It took two and a half years for Indian

immigration to gain strength, but by the autumn of 1906 it had become, in the eyes of British Columbians, an invasion. From August until December, almost every C.P.R. liner brought Indians by the hundreds—696 on the *Tartar* in mid-November—and they kept coming in spite of a daunting reception.

Lumber companies and railway contractors wanted them; the fruit growers of the Okanagan wanted them; but local politicians, dancing to the tune of the Trades and Labour Council, were hostile, and the press supported a vicious and uninformed campaign exemplified by the front-page headline: 'Hindus Cover Dead Bodies with Butter'.[6] The mayor of Vancouver posted police around the immigration shed on the waterfront to prevent new arrivals from stepping off C.P.R. property before they could be moved directly out of the city to jobs in the interior. But they came drifting back anyway. Late in November, the South Vancouver civic authorities, acting on the complaints of a few citizens, descended on a number of Indians living in old shacks and threw them out into the cold. A few days later, the mayor of Vancouver began to round up Indians crowded into condemned buildings throughout the city to move them to Eburne, well out of the city. There they were housed at their own expense—$3.00 per head per month—in an abandoned cannery with no running water, hastily fixed up with a few stoves and electric lights. No level of government or, for that matter, no charitable organization would accept responsibility for the welfare of these immigrants. Instead, they were harassed by the police when they wandered the streets of Vancouver or tried to camp in the parks.

The immigrants endured the worst of their hardships with a stoicism that most Vancouverites did not understand, and, by pooling their resources, and with the help of a couple of former British residents of India in Vancouver who took an interest in their plight, they stuck it out. Two thousand had arrived during the latter half of 1906. By the end of December, with the exception of some 300 who had taken steamers for Seattle and San Francisco, all but fifty or sixty had found employment in British Columbia, most of them in saw mills.[7] The authorities would gladly have deported any convicted of vagrancy, but there were few such cases; those who were out of work were looked after by their companions, and, despite the predictions of the Vancouver City Council, none became a public charge. In their own way they had adapted to conditions in British Columbia, although their presence was not accepted, and the press and the public were prepared to believe the worst charges against them.

Politicians and labour leaders in British Columbia had campaigned against oriental immigration since C.P.R. contractors had imported Chinese coolies in the 1870's and 1880's. They reacted swiftly when the trickle of Indians first began and they felt considerable frustration when the Dominion government would not admit there was a problem. Sir Wilfred Laurier, Prime Minister from 1896 to 1911, made few friends in British Columbia when he suggested that Canada could not exclude British subjects of any kind or race. In 1907, as oriental immigration rose while the economy went into a temporary decline, the Vancouver Trades and Labour Council spawned an Asiatic Exclusion League linked to anti-oriental leagues in California. The president was a member of the Bartenders Union, but the League drew support from prominent professional men and politicians.[8] In September, a parade organized by the League became a riot after *provocateurs* directed marchers through the Chinese and Japanese quarters. Impressed at last, Laurier moved to check Japanese and Indian immigration.

The Japanese government, in a gentleman's agreement similar to one negotiated with the United States, promised to limit Japanese emigration to Canada to 400 a year. But the same undertaking could not be obtained from the government of British India who were afraid that Indian nationalists would find a way to exploit the issue. What kind of an Empire was it that did not allow free movement of its subject people? The Viceroy and his Council did not question Canada's right to close the door. In fact they hoped she would because they could see that an Indian community in North America would always be a source of disquieting ideas at home.[9] All they asked was that discrimination be disguised, and, respecting this wish, Laurier's government drafted two ingenious orders-in-council, one requiring that all Asian immigrants entering Canada possess at least $200, and the other prohibiting the landing of any immigrant who came other than by a continuous passage. The former constituted a substantial barrier to men who might earn with difficulty ten or twenty cents a day in their own country; the latter was made effective by pressuring steamship companies not to provide a Canada-

India service or to sell through tickets from Indian ports. Both were designed only against Indians. They were issued in 1908, and they brought Sikh immigration to an abrupt halt.

By this time, 6,000 Indians had landed in Canada, although many were no longer in the country. Those who arrived in 1907, in the midst of a slump, had great difficulty finding work or shelter. Seven hundred or more were still unemployed the following summer. They were living in run-down houses and shacks in the city and in the woods beyond the city limits, and would come daily into the downtown area, knocking on back doors, asking for work and begging for money. Many of their friends had moved across the border into Washington and Oregon. By the summer and autumn of 1908 a number had found their way to the agricultural valleys of California where they could get outdoor work picking grapes and oranges, hoeing beans and asparagus, or thinning and topping beets. By 1913, there were three times as many Sikhs in the United States as in Canada, most of them on the fruit ranches and in the small towns of the Sacramento Valley. This development had not gone unnoticed, and from 1908 the American Bureau of Immigration was under pressure to keep the Sikhs out. Large numbers were turned back on the grounds that they were likely to become public charges 'because of the unfavourable attitude of the people of the Pacific Coast States', an extraordinary application of American law.[10]

For those who stayed in Canada, circumstances improved after 1907–8. In Vancouver in 1908 and in Victoria in 1912 they built temples which were meeting places and refuges, open, in the Sikh tradition, to anyone, Hindu, Christian, Muslim, or Sikh. Yet the Sikhs and their fellow Indians remained separate from the larger community in which they lived and, with reason, felt isolated and under attack. Those who had served in the British Indian army or in the police forces of Singapore, Hong Kong, or Shanghai, who had been trained by English officers and who knew some English were at least not bashful in the presence of a European and generally created a good impression. But half of the immigrants had come to North America directly from rural areas where they had learned neither to read nor write their own languages, let alone speak English. They were lost outside their own community, and they lived among Europeans and worked for them without addressing them or establishing any personal contact, depending on a few of their number who could speak English to deal with the outside world. With nowhere to go for entertainment, they would gather downtown to socialize. Standing around in groups on Powell Street, or Main Street, they were conspicuous, and that, as much as anything, kept alive public prejudice against them.

They were mostly peaceful men, more likely—living in substandard housing—to have trouble with the health inspector than with the police. Yet they were aware of Canadian hostility, and they saw evidence of persecution, not just in the immigration law which prevented their friends and relatives from entering the country, or in the speed with which the British Columbia provincial assembly moved to deny them the right to vote, but in their daily encounters with the authorities. They knew that the Canadian government would happily remove the whole community if it could find the means. In the autumn of 1908 when many were jobless they had been 'invited' to go to British Honduras where, they were told, there was a demand for their labour. J. B. Harkin, private secretary to the Minister of the Interior, accompanied by Hopkinson, took two delegates to see the Honduras for themselves. When these delegates returned with unfavourable reports, immigration officials warned the Sikhs that if they did not go, and were found vagrant, they would be deported. It sounded like a threat, and in response they had organized themselves for mutual support so that the authorities would not have an excuse to lay hands on a single one of them.[11]

These men harboured bitter feelings against their own government. They saw that the Japanese were better treated than they were, and they shared the conviction that because they were *kale admi*—black men—they were the stepchildren of the Empire. The condition of Indians in Natal and the Transvaal, where Gandhi struggled, proved the point. Discriminatory legislation in Australia and New Zealand drove it home. Their own government, the *sircar-ma-bap*—literally the 'mother-father' government of India—was indifferent to their plight and did not look after them as the Government of Japan did the Japanese.

They would not have talked this way in the Panjab where their landlords and headmen supported the government; where their shrines were controlled by priests who depended on the government; and where the Singh Sabha associations, which stood for pure Sikhism, and the Chief Khalsa Diwan, the principal political voice of the Sikhs, both promoted loyalty to the government. Ever since the Mutiny of 1857, the British had taken Sikhs in preference to Hindus and Muslims for the army and civil service. They had encouraged the separatist feelings of the Sikh minority —twelve per cent of the Panjab population in 1911—distinguishing between Hindu and Sikh for official purposes when many Hindus and Sikhs were themselves careless about the difference, and establishing Sikh regiments in which the unshorn hair, comb, breeches, bangle, and sword of the baptized Sikh—the *kesh*, *kangha*, *kaccha*, *kara*, and *kirpan*—were not merely permitted but required. Sikhism, its apparent strength declining in the latter half of the nineteenth century, had been revitalized and its leadership bound to the British regime. If there were any contrary influences, they did not reach the villages where British authority was accepted as indisputable and even divinely ordained.

In British Columbia and other colonies overseas, Sikh emigrants mixed with men who attacked British rule and preached revolution—men who could not return to India for fear of the police and who waged war from abroad; men like Taraknath Das, who had espoused the extremist cause when he was a nineteen-year-old student at Calcutta University, and who had played a leading role in the formation of the *Dacca Anusilan Samiti*, a secret revolutionary society born in the midst of the nationalist agitation which swept Bengal in 1905-6. In January 1908, Taraknath opened a school for Sikh emigrants at Millside, New Westminster, near Vancouver. Hopkinson put a spotlight on him a few months later, going to the British and Canadian press with the story that the seditious movement in India was being directed from the Pacific Coast of North America and that Millside was a centre of revolutionary activity. His action forced the Canadian authorities to close the school. Taraknath moved to Seattle, but that was not the end of his activity among Indians in British Columbia.[12]

Hopkinson at that time had no official position in Canada. He had turned up in Vancouver in 1908, twenty-eight years of age, an Inspector of the Calcutta Metropolitan police with four years' experience, officially on leave, but pursuing investigations for the Criminal Intelligence Deparment in India.[13] He was soon known to the Minister of the Interior and it was not long before he was taken on by the Immigration Branch, nicely placed to keep a watch on men like Taraknath.

Working hand-in-glove with Taraknath was Guran Ditta Kumar, a native of Bannu on the North-West Frontier of India, at one time an apprentice to an Indian photographer in Rawalpindi, and briefly an instructor in Hindi and Urdu at the National College in Calcutta. It was in Calcutta, where he stayed at Maratha Lodge, a boarding house marked by the C.I.D. as a gathering place for revolutionaries, that Kumar first met Taraknath, and it was with Taraknath's help that he set up a grocery store in Victoria soon after his arrival in October 1907. In Vancouver, in December 1909, Kumar opened the *Swadesh Sewak* (Servant of the Country) Home, a meeting place and shelter for revolutionaries masked as a night school in English and mathematics for Sikh immigrants. Both Taraknath and Kumar had their eyes on Sikh troops in India whose loyalty they tried to shake with accounts of the treatment that their brethren received in Canada. For a period Taraknath published an English-language paper, *Free Hindustan*, in which he tried to address himself to the Sikhs. Kumar took up the task more effectively in the *Swadesh Sewak* published monthly in Gurmukhi, the written language of the Sikhs, and sent back to India in bulk until the Indian government was alerted and put it on a prohibited list in March 1911.[14]

While under Canadian law there was not much that Hopkinson could do against Kumar and his friends, he served the Indian government by passing on every scrap of information he could command. It was through him that the C.I.D. built up their files on Taraknath Das, Kumar, and other Indian activists in Canada and the United States. It was through names and addresses that he supplied that the C.I.D. traced literature such as *Swadesh Sewak* when it entered India. Local Indians knew that Hopkinson was a secret-service man; yet they were not particularly discreet even when he turned up at their public meetings bringing a stenographer to whom he dictated a translation of everything that was said. Instead they assumed the offensive, demanding that he be dismissed and replaced because he did not know their language—he was fluent in Hindi but less certain in Panjabi and the Gurmukhi script of the Sikhs—and, when that failed, charging him with extorting money from Indians entering Canada from the United States, an accusation that was investigated and dismissed.[15]

Kumar left Vancouver in the spring of 1913 bound for Manila, a strategic base, he thought, for revolutionary work among Sikhs in the Far East. By that time, he had been eclipsed locally by Chagan Kairaj Varma, a 48-year-old Hindu from Porbandar State in Gujarat. This man had lived for a number of years in Japan before running into financial trouble and absconding to Honolulu under the Muslim name of Husain Rahim. That was the name he used in Canada. He had entered the country as a tourist in January 1910, having arrived at Vancouver on the S.S. *Moana* from Honolulu with a first-class railway ticket to Montreal; and he had been arrested and ordered deported nine months later after he had returned to Vancouver, gone into business, and applied for permission to stay. At the police station, he was searched and from his pocket was plucked a notebook in which he had scrawled a recipe for manufacturing nitroglycerine and the addresses of Indian activists in the United States, France, Natal, and elsewhere. Hopkinson had interviewed him when he first landed; Hopkinson was there when he was arrested; and he had turned on the Inspector with vehemence: 'You drive us Hindus out of Canada and we will drive every white man out of India.' But Hopkinson was not able to drive him out. Rahim went to the courts and won. The judges found that the immigration official had not followed proper procedures, and that victory over the Immigration Branch gave him a special standing among the Indians in Vancouver.

Rahim ran the Canada India Supply & Trust Company, an incorporated company trading in Vancouver and suburban real estate. His clients were Sikh millworkers, and like other Hindu businessmen—storekeepers and labour contractors—who had set up shop in Vancouver, he had a stake in the community. In different circumstances, he might have followed a cautious course. But he was an activist first and a real-estate agent second and there was nothing in the Canadian situation to make it otherwise. He did not disguise his low opinion of the Canadian government and the 'servile' Canadian press, and he was bold enough to stand up at a public meeting to say that the Japanese were being admitted to preserve peace and that to get redress in Canada 'we must go back to India with a petition where we are 330 millions strong.'[17] He talked of pressurizing the Indian legislature, but he was not afraid to state openly that he thought that Indians would not be protected overseas until they had secured self-government at home.

Hopkinson associated Rahim, Kumar, and Taraknath Das with the advocates of the bomb and the pistol. The evidence against Kumar and Taraknath was substantial; Rahim was judged by the company he kept. The *Dacca Anusilan Samiti*, in which Taraknath had once been active, had been smashed by the Bengal police in 1910 and thirty-six of its members charged with terrorist crimes—murder, attempted murder, and theft. Taraknath, the C.I.D. had determined, was a contributor to *Bande Mataram* published in Geneva by Mrs Bhikaiji Rustom Cama, a leading figure among Indian revolutionaries in Europe. He was also in close contact with Har Dayal, a former editor of *Bande Mataram* now living in Palo Alto, California, and lecturing in Indian philosophy at Stanford University.

The language of these people was not pretty. 'It is no infamy if an Indian pupil shoots down his English professor, if an Indian clerk shoots down his English superior, if an Indian barrister shoots down the English Judge and an Indian patient shoots down an English doctor,' ran one piece in *Bande Mataram*. 'In a meeting or in a bungalow, on a railway or in a carriage, in a shop or in a church, in a garden or at a fair, whenever the opportunity comes, Englishmen ought to be killed.'[18] In December 1912, during a state procession in Delhi, a terrorist had thrown a bomb at the Viceroy, wounding him and killing an attendant. The police uncovered evidence connecting Har Dayal with one of the suspects, and, while he was not directly involved, he extolled the deed in a pamphlet prepared as soon as he received the news. It was, he wrote, 'one of the sweetest and loveliest bombs that have exploded in India ... one of the most serviceable and successful bombs in the History of Freedom all over the world.'[19]

In the United States Har Dayal could—for the moment—publish propaganda like this with impunity. In India he would have been silenced quickly enough. Hopkinson went down to San Francisco in January 1913, checked into a hotel under an assumed name, and asked the British Consul-General to safeguard his papers 'should he come to harm.' He spent three weeks on

Har Dayal's trail, attending his lectures, seeking evidence that he could use to get him deported. But, while he proved to himself that Har Dayal was an extremely dangerous man and a potential influence over the 100 Indian students on the Stanford and Berkeley campuses, he produced nothing that American officials would act on.[20]

Har Dayal, Taraknath, Kumar, Rahim, and most of their activist friends were clean-shaven, educated, Westernized Hindus far removed in outlook from the Sikh immigrants with whom they worked. There was, among the more orthodox Sikhs at least, little inclination to follow the lead of outsiders. Consequently, there was no organization in Vancouver that could speak for the whole Indian community. The Sikhs had their own assembly, the Khalsa Diwan, and only the more liberal among them would participate in the United India League founded by Kumar and Taraknath. Many were wary of any action that would lead to trouble with the authorities—afraid, at one point, to send a delegation to London lest it offend the Canadians. A solid core of veterans looked back on their service with pride and wore their decorations without apology. Rahim dismissed them as 'a few of the "war dogs" utilized by the British to kill Chinamen in Hong Kong', but their attitude was certainly an obstacle to united action.[21]

When the Governor-General visited Vancouver in September 1912, a good many of these 'war dogs' were in the crowds, sporting medals, at odds with the President of the Khalsa Diwan, the priest Bhag Singh, who had rejected an invitation for Sikhs to take part in a military review. Bhag Singh, a five-year veteran of the Tenth Bengal Lancer Regiment, had burned his honourable discharge certificate in 1909—three years after he immigrated to Canada—to make the point that service in the British Indian army was the service of slavery. He and the other executive officers of the Khalsa Diwan had joined with Rahim and Kumar in the formation of a special branch of the Vancouver-based Socialist Party of Canada, assimilating, in a half-digested way, the language of class warfare.[22] They were militant, even though a large part of the Sikh community was not.

There were, or had been, more moderate spokesmen, although none recognized as moderate by the immigration people. From the time he arrived in Vancouver in 1908, until his support de-

clined in 1912, the acknowledged leader was Teja Singh, an
educated Amritsar Sikh (M.A. Lahore, L.L.B. Cambridge, A.M.
Harvard).[23] His teaching was more theosophical than political.
He was, Rahim would say, one of the Illusionists who 'resign
their world in favour of Britishers, and turn to seek salvation'.
At the same time, he had given practical direction, organizing
a kind of workingmen's society to provide relief and founding
the Guru Nanak Mining and Trust Company to manage invest-
ments. In the beginning, sixty or seventy Sikhs had promised to
take care of his expenses as long as he stayed in Vancouver, but
by 1912 they were no longer willing to do so. The issue came
to a head when Bhag Singh and his fellow priest Balwant Singh
(Singh, meaning Lion, the baptismal name of all male followers
of Guru Gobind Singh) tried to bring their families into Canada.

Balwant Singh had gone back to India in 1909; Bhag Singh in
1910. They returned with their wives and Balwant's two small
children, leaving Calcutta early in 1911. In Calcutta, Rangoon,
and Hong Kong they were unable to get passages to Canada—
that was how the continuous passage regulation worked—and
when they tried to enter at San Francisco and then Seattle they
were turned back. Late in the year they found themselves again
in Hong Kong, where Bhag Singh's wife gave birth to a child
conceived some time after they had started out. Their attempts
to enter at American ports had been supported and publicized by
Taraknath Das and other agitators and Indians in North America
were well aware of their situation. At this point, Teja Singh led
a delegation to Ottawa where he met with the Minister of the
Interior in late November and in December. He came back to
Vancouver announcing that the Minister had given way and that
wives and children would be admitted. His triumphant news went
back to Hong Kong, and a month later Bhag Singh, Balwant
Singh, and their families arrived at Vancouver on the S.S.
Monteagle.

The two men, having been in Canada before, were landed. But
the women and the three small children were detained and ordered
deported, and then released on $2,000 bail pending an appeal to
the Minister. It was obvious to everyone that Teja Singh had accomplished nothing, although his mission to Ottawa had cost the
community $1,500. There was a lot of grumbling about that. Some
men wanted to bring over wives themselves; all were incensed

because the Canadian government was splitting up the families of two priests; and, as long as those families were threatened, the community was kept in an uproar. At the same time, the Women's National Council, claiming to represent 400 local women, and the Ministerial Association of Vancouver both opposed the admission of Indian women, and that was a good measure of the state of opinion in the host population. It was the C.I.D. man, Hopkinson, seeking to take the issue away from the two priests, who suggested that the Minister should allow the two women and their children to stay while making it clear that other Indians could not expect the same concession. He did not think that the radicals would be able to keep an agitation going after that because there was so little hope of reform among the majority of their people. But the issue had already dragged on for six months and in the meantime Bhag Singh, Balwant Singh, and their friends had cut into the ranks of the conservative and uncommitted. The whole affair cost Teja Singh his standing and he shortly left the city to return to India.[24]

After Teja Singh was gone, Dr Sundar Singh was the only moderate with pretensions to leadership. In 1909, Sundar Singh had managed to enter the country at Halifax where immigration officials were less vigilant. He had edited the *Aryan*, an English-language paper which appeared briefly in 1911; and he later managed to put out a number of issues of the *Sansar* published in Victoria in Gurmukhi and advertised as the only Indian-language paper in Canada. He had his own organization, the Hindustanee Association, of which he seemed to be the only member, and he and L. W. Hall, a Presbyterian missionary converted, it was said, to the Sikh religion, were the principal figures in the Hindu Friend Society of Victoria. Sundar Singh and Hall had gone to Ottawa with Teja Singh in November 1911; Sundar Singh went back again in the spring of 1913, and he continued to parade before Canadian officials and the Canadian public as a representative of the Indians in British Columbia. But it all seemed to be empty posturing; he wanted to be important, but he had few friends; his countrymen trusted him no more than he trusted them; he was so secretive that none of Hopkinson's informants could find out where he had come from; and when he tried to speak for the whole community, Canadian officials quite rightly paid him little attention.[25]

For the radicals the problem was not Sundar Singh, but the servility, pessimism, and indifference of so many of the immigrants. They had come to North America to make money and in the pursuit of work they were persistent, even desperate. If there was the chance of a job, the unemployed among them would wait at the gates for hours and days. In California it was not uncommon for Sikhs to try to force themselves on employers by entering fields and beginning to work without being asked. They would endure a lot to achieve their objective. They were, Har Dayal said, 'timid, shabby, and ignorant'. The hope was that they could be lifted to 'a higher level of thought and action'.[26] Bhag Singh played on their sense of duty. 'You have made a lot of money in this country,' he told a meeting called on behalf of a number of immigrants who were being deported from the United States, 'and now is the time to spend some to assist your brothers. . . .'[27]

2

ENCOURAGEMENT

In autumn 1913, Hopkinson's watch on the Pacific Coast appeared more important than ever. Har Dayal had been active all spring and summer, touring Washington, Oregon, and California, drumming up support for a new organization, the Hindu Association of the Pacific Coast. It was no use talking about American citizenship and immigration laws, he told Sikhs at meeting after meeting. They had to strike at the British because the British were to blame for the way Indians were treated in America. Under his leadership, 1324 Valencia Street, San Francisco, became the most vital centre for Indian revolutionary work, eclipsing Madame Cama's *Abinav Bharat* (New India) Society in Paris. Har Dayal modelled his organization on what he had known among Indians in London and Paris a few years before. The Hindu Association, open to anyone, was the base from which members were drawn into the *Ghadr* (Mutiny) Party and the more select *Yugantar* (New Era) *Ashram*. No one was admitted into the Party except on the recommendation of an inner circle; no one was to be told the secrets or confidential business of the *Ashram* until he had worked there for six months; anyone who betrayed those secrets or stole from the *Ashram* was to be killed. The intent was there even if the organization did not work with such deadly efficiency in practice.[1]

In the initial phase, the work of the *Ghadr* party was propaganda. On 1 November 1913, Har Dayal, as editor and publisher, brought out the first issue of the *Ghadr*, a weekly in Urdu and Gurmukhi. The leading article explained the purpose. 'What is our name? Mutiny. What is our work? Mutiny. Where will this mutiny break out? In India. When will it break out? In a few years. Why should it break out? Because the people can no longer bear the oppression and tyranny practised under British

rule and are ready to fight and die for freedom.'² The *Ghadr*
went out to members of the Hindu Association and it was read
to meetings of Sikh workers up and down the coast. Bhag Singh
read it out in the Sikh Temple in Vancouver. Those who listened
were told to send money to the *Yugantar Ashram* so that thousands of copies of the *Ghadr* could be published. They were to
remember what they read in the *Ghadr* and to make others read
it; and when they were finished they were to send their copies
to India in ordinary envelopes.

The British Consul-General in San Francisco was aware of what
was going on and so were the American immigration officials.³
The meetings of the Hindu Association had been openly publicized; and, although literature had been put into the mail with
false originating addresses, much of it had been intercepted. It had
been decided, weeks before the first appearance of the *Ghadr*,
that Hopkinson should spend the winter in the San Francisco
area. (He planned to rent his house in Vancouver and to take his
English wife and two children with him for the period November
to February.) And, judging that Hopkinson was going to be
busier than ever, the immigration agent at Vancouver asked permission to take on another interpreter.

Hopkinson intended to get away from Vancouver on 1 November, but his departure was delayed. Five months earlier he had
allowed Bhagwan Singh Jakh, a revolutionary of the stature of
Har Dayal, to slip into the country right under his nose. Bhagwan
Singh was a man of about thirty from the village of Viring in
the district of Jullunder.⁴ He had been involved in disturbances
in the Panjab in 1907 and had left India the following year to
escape arrest. For three years he had been chief priest of the Sikh
gurdwara (temple) in Hong Kong, and for most of that time he
had kept the Sikh colony there in turmoil. Twice he had been
arrested for preaching sedition to Sikh troops, and finally in May
1913, he had been forced out of the colony altogether. A few
weeks later he arrived at Victoria, on the Canadian Pacific steamer
Empress of Russia, carrying another man's identity. He had been
coached on his answers and he had been able to convince Hopkinson that he was Natha Singh, a Sikh with established residence
in Canada.

Bhagwan Singh was a powerful speaker. His words came in a
torrent rich in imagery. Hopkinson, standing at the back of a

meeting, translating to a stenographer, would find Bhagwan Singh's language beyond him to translate. On arrival in Vancouver, Bhagwan Singh began lecturing at weekly meetings in the *gurdwara*, urging his listeners to adopt the *Bande Mataram* (Hail Mother) greeting of the Bengali extremists as a mark of unity with other Indians. The Sikhs in Canada, he said, should go back to India to join in the struggle against the British; and, when he said that, Bhag Singh and other activists would stand up and promise to do so.[5] The excitement he generated did not pass unnoticed for a minute, but it was no easy matter for the immigration authorities to produce witnesses against him, and it was not until September 30 when the *Empress of Russia* was back in Vancouver, and the Chinese steerage steward available to testify, that Bhagwan Singh was arrested and ordered deported. Even then his lawyer appealed to the Minister and managed to obtain a re-hearing for him so he remained free on bail.

The case was still in the air when the Japanese liner *Panama Maru* docked at Victoria on 17 October with fifty-six Indians, more than had been seen on any liner since 1908. Hopkinson now knew that several men had duped him besides Bhagwan Singh, and he gathered that local Indians had written home encouraging others to try. After he had finished with the people on the *Panama Maru*, he knew it for a fact.

All fifty-six Indians on the *Panama Maru* said they had been in Canada before and most of them carried documents of some kind or other—tax receipts, receipts for money orders, time cards, deeds, agreements for sale—as proof.[6] As it turned out, they had picked up these pieces of paper from Calcutta and Hong Kong in place of more official documents which simply could not be obtained. The Vancouver immigration office, as a rule, had refused to give identification to Indians intending to go home for a visit—not to prevent them from leaving, but to make it more difficult to come back. If the immigration officials had been sure they could get away with it, they would have refused to admit any Indian with or without previous domicile in Canada. But the law on lost domicile was unclear and they were afraid of losing face if the courts went against them. Since they had not given out official certificates, they had to accept other kinds of verification.

When Hopkinson recognized a man, there was no problem,

and he allowed seventeen of the fifty-six to go ashore. But he found the others doubtful and they were locked up in the Immigration Hall. Three days passed—a Sunday, a holiday and a day spent at a re-hearing of Bhagwan Singh's case—before Hopkinson returned to Victoria. When he did, he found that the detained men had changed stories. Only one said that he was a returning resident, and the rest would not admit they had made such a claim. They said Hopkinson had got it wrong. They were brought before a Board of Inquiry—three immigration officers—where they were represented by a lawyer hired by their friends in Victoria and Vancouver.

During the hearings the lawyer asked one of them if he had told Hopkinson the truth. He replied that he had taken the advice of an Indian in Hong Kong, 'You say just as I am telling you and you will be landed.'[7] When this did not work he decided to stick to the facts. The others were not so honest, but it did not make any difference because they were all ordered deported.

It was the furore over Bhagwan Singh and the passengers of the *Panama Maru* which kept Hopkinson in Vancouver after 1 November. Indians had come up to him during Bhagwan Singh's second hearing threatening to get witnesses to say he had taken bribes. It was an old tactic and he immediately warned his superiors. 'I am one man against the whole colony', he complained.[8] Rahim and Bhag Singh were making the most of the opportunity. They wanted to help Bhagwan Singh and they wanted to overthrow the Canadian immigration barrier. At the same time, it was worthwhile fighting in the courts if, in the process, they could stir up the Sikhs in Canada and at home.

The lawyer they turned to was J. Edward Bird, a man Rahim had met among Socialists in Vancouver, an experienced but by no means outstanding advocate in his mid-forties. Getting a case into court was no easy matter because section twenty-three of the revised Immigration Act of 1910 said that no court or judge could interfere with a decision of a Board of Inquiry. Bird gave notice of appeal to the Minister of the Interior—the only appeal allowed—but he also went to Mr Justice Murphy in Victoria with an application for a writ of *habeas corpus*, arguing that the orders-in-council cited by the Board of Inquiry—the continuous passage order and the $200 requirement order—did not conform to the Act. *Origin* was used instead of *race, native or citizen* instead of the more specific *native or naturalized citizen,* and *actual personal possession of $200* instead of *possession in one's own right.* Murphy did not see the argument, although he did say that the courts had a right to step in if it could be shown that the orders-in-council were faulty. The government lawyer had contended that the courts had no jurisdiction whatsoever.

Bird appealed to the Chief Justice of the British Columbia Supreme Court, Gordon Hunter, who saw merit where Murphy did not and granted a test case. At this point the immigration officials realized that they were probably going to lose and it rankled. It showed in the behaviour of Hopkinson's superior, Malcolm R. J. Reid, the Vancouver immigration agent, a political appointee like most immigration officers in Canada at that time —a Conservative party hack who had been an elementary school teacher until he was given the immigration agency following the Conservative election victory of 1911. Reid owed his job to the local Conservative M.P., H. H. Stevens, a rabid opponent of Indian immigration, and he acted like Stevens' minion, regularly sending him copies of the material on Indians that went over his desk. When Stevens complained because Indians had published letters in one of the local papers, Reid went around to the editors of the two Conservative dailies and got them to stop their columns.[9] That was how the two worked. In Hopkinson Indians encountered the long arm of the Indian government, but in Reid and Stevens they ran into local prejudice pure and simple.

Bhagwan Singh had been free on bail pending the Minister's decision on his appeal, and his lawyer, Bird, armed with an order for a writ of *habeas corpus,* had been ready to spring him loose once bail expired. As soon as the Minister's verdict was given out, Malcolm Reid called the priest around, supposedly to renew bail. But, when he arrived, he was released, given his $2,000 bail money, and then, as he turned to go, arrested, handcuffed, and bundled onto the afternoon ferry for Victoria.

One of Bird's law partners dashed around to a British Columbia Supreme Court judge, interrupting him during a sitting of the criminal assizes, and got him to send a wireless message stating that a writ had been issued. But Reid would not recognize the order. At Victoria, Bhagwan Singh was taken to the wharf where the *Empress of Japan* was preparing to sail for Yokohama and Hong Kong, and, after a tremendous struggle which cost one policeman a bit of an ear and another a slice of his hand, pushed up the gangway. Minutes before the ship was due to depart, Bird rushed up with a second writ and Captain Dixon Hopcroft of the *Empress* called Bhagwan Singh up to the deck, showed him the gangway, and told him he could go. For the length of the gang-way he was a free man. But at the shoreline he ran into Reid and a wall of police who overpowered him and dragged him back onto the boat. All this was witnessed by a crowd of Sikhs on the wharf who were restrained by a dozen Victoria policemen. Bhagwan Singh was locked in a cabin. The captain refused to hold the ship any longer, and the *Empress* cast off.

It would have been better, said a Vancouver lawyer who knew something of the situation, for Reid 'to have unlawfully deported a hundred ordinary Hindus than this priest, Bhagwan Singh'.[10] The immigration agent had pitted himself against the whole Indian community; he had given ammunition to Rahim and his friends; and he had done it simply to show his authority. Rahim had boasted that his people always won in the courts and Reid had answered with force. He and Stevens made what they could of the fact that Bhagwan Singh was a seditionist. But, by snatching him in defiance of two writs, without giving him time to pick up his personal effects, they had made a martyr of him and given sedition a boost.

Five days later, on 24 November, thirty-eight of the *Panama Maru* Sikhs, packed into a street car and escorted by mounted police, came from the Immigration Hall to the Victoria Court House. (One was missing. He apparently got a bar loose in the Immigration Hall and was able to squeeze through a window and slide down a pipe. The others could have escaped as easily, but were determined to have their day in court and kept an eye on each other.) A couple of hundred Sikhs stood threateningly out-side the Court House while the lawyers argued inside. Late in the afternoon the Chief Justice gave his ruling. The orders-in-council went beyond the Act and were invalid: *asiatic origin* was not an alternative for *asiatic race*, because it was more inclusive, covering Europeans born in India as well as Indians; *actual personal posses-sion* was not the same as *possession in one's own right*, because it meant you had to have the money on your person and could not satisfy an immigration officer with proof that you had it in the bank; and *natives or citizens* could not be substituted for *native or naturalized citizen* because *native* was a broader term than *native citizen.*

The government lawyer had argued that these men were guilty of misrepresentation; they had lied when first examined by Hopkinson; and that was reason also for deporting them. But Chief Justice Hunter did not find this charge clearly set out in the deportation order and rejected it. The court was free to intervene, he said, because the orders-in-council had not been issued in accordance with the Act, and he ordered the release of all the Sikhs except four who were being deported on medical grounds.

A narrow, technical interpretation of a few key-words—an interpretation that most of Hunter's brethren on the bench would not have accepted—had carried the day. It had carried the day in the court of a Chief Justice who, in the past, had more than once presided drunk, who had been an embarrassment to the government that appointed him and to political friends who felt bound to support him.[11] But it was an interpretation that, nonetheless, left immigraion officials without any legal recourse. To add to the injury, the four men rejected for medical reasons ran away an hour after they were brought back to the Immigration Hall. The special officer on duty, thinking that rats might get at a sack of flour used by the Sikhs for cooking, had gone down to the basement to get it. When he came back up he found a hole in the wire work on one side of the exercise balcony, and the four gone, while a block away a second officer just off duty stared at a car speeding off at forty kilometres an hour.

The Superintendent of Immigration had talked of fighting in the higher courts if necessary, but when he looked into the matter he found it could not be done. Under the law of British Columbia, the applicant for a writ of *habeas corpus* was the only party with an appeal. The only recourse for the government was to rescind the faulty orders and to replace them with new orders that accorded better with the Act. The cabinet discussed the situation on 1 December and on several days following without doing anything, waiting until officials had a chance to study Hunter's written opinion. As a stop-gap, an order was issued on 8 December prohibiting the landing at any British Columbia port of entry of any artisan or labourer, skilled or unskilled, up to 31 March.

The issue blew up at a time of high unemployment and generated extra excitement for that reason. The Premier of British

Columbia, Sir Richard McBride, called it 'a critical state of affairs'. The Vancouver *Province* said that the Hindu problem had assumed 'a most serious and menacing aspect'.[12] Only thirty-nine Sikhs had entered the country, but reading the Vancouver papers one gathered that much more was afoot than that. Much of the reaction was for Ottawa's benefit, to get the cabinet moving, and nobody made more than H. H. Stevens. 'I threw out a challenge in Toronto and I throw it out there,' he told a Vancouver audience. 'I challenge any man living to bring out a single instance in the whole history of the Indian nation to show that their civilization has done anything at all to uplift the other races of the world. I say their civilization is unproductive of good to the human race as a whole.'[13]

Rahim and his people were in a dangerous mood, elated by their victory, but expressing dark sentiments about the treatment of Bhagwan Singh. Stevens, answering a clergyman's question— if Christ appeared on Granville Street wearing a turban, would he be reported to immigration and thrown out of the country?— had said that Christ would not come preaching virulent sedition. Rahim picked this up, remarking that Christ had been crucified on just such a charge. 'If the immigration officer had gone further and done to Bhai Bhagwan Singh what the Jews did to Christ... Mr Stevens would have been satisfied.'[14] But there was worse to be said about certain Sikhs who had gone running to Hopkinson when Bhagwan Singh had begun to lecture. The *Ghadr* took this up in its fifth issue, warning that the disloyal party in Canada was very strong. A meeting was held at the *gurdwara* in Vancouver late in December and a poem was read naming three men— Bela Singh, Baboo Singh, and Ganga Ram—and calling for their destruction along with Hopkinson and Reid. Rahim, presiding, said that he hoped and requested that someone would 'fix' these men; and one of his friends, Munsha Singh—contemptuously known by the Muslim name, Abdullah, because he had shaved his beard—told the assembly that no nation could survive which did not do away with its traitors. A lot of men present did not like what they heard and ten of them went around to the immigration office to report on what had happened.[15]

After the victory in Hunter's court, Canadian Sikhs wrote home saying, 'Get a ticket and board a ship and we will see that you land in Vancouver.'[16] Some took Hunter's decision to mean that the Canadian government could not stop Indian immigration. Others understood that it was only a matter of time before the opening was closed and urged friends and relatives to come while they could. There were already a large number of Sikhs in Hong Kong, Shanghai, and Manila looking for some way to get to North America. Many had left the Panjab hoping to enter the United States by way of the Philippines. But this back door had been closed in August by American immigration officials at San Francisco, who had stopped twenty-two Indians even though they had come from what was an American territorial possession. Hundreds—some said thousands—of Sikhs waited in Manila and other ports in the Far East for the judgment of a California District Court, but when it came down on 5 December—eleven days after Hunter's decision—it upheld the immigration officers.[17] That made the news from Canada doubly important.

On 27 December, Daniel Keefe, former chief of the American Immigration Service, stepped out of his Hong Kong hotel for a stroll and struck up a conversation with two Sikhs he met at a crossing. One of them showed him a letter prepared on behalf of six hundred Sikhs in Hong Kong for forwarding to their friends in America. 'For God's sake,' it read, 'help us to get to the United States or Canada, the new Canadian law will go into effect on 15 March, 1914 [this was not quite true, but close enough] after which time few Hindus will be admitted into Canada. It has been much more difficult for the past six months to get into Manila than heretofore. We are shut out of Australia and New Zealand. For God's sake come to our assistance so that we will be able to get into the United States or Canada.'[18]

The only steamship companies operating between the Far East and British Columbia, the Canadian Pacific, the Blue Funnel Line, and the Osaka Shosen Kaisha—the Japanese line that owned the *Panama Maru*—would not sell tickets to Sikhs. They knew that they would have trouble with the Canadian authorities if they did.[19]

3

DEPARTURE

Gurdit Singh was fifty-five in 1913: an old man of good appearance, white-bearded, with smiling eyes, patriarchal, a self-taught, self-made man. His father, Hookum Singh, still living in the village of Sirhali where Gurdit Singh was born, was a farmer; and farming, as practised on his father's few acres of irrigated land, was what Gurdit Singh knew for the first eighteen or twenty years of his life. When he was six, he briefly attended a religious school in his village, until he had a misunderstanding with the priest and stubbornly refused to go back. When he was eleven or twelve and ashamed because he could not write a letter to his father who had gone to Malaya—in hard times in a year of drought—he got hold of a primer and taught himself. In 1875 his brother went to Malaya and he later followed, having been rejected for the army as too thin in the chest by a regimental recruiting officer in Ambala. He worked for a Chinese pork-dealer in Taiping, learning Chinese and Malay in the process, and then started a dairy supplying the Sikh regiment stationed there. As a side line he imported cattle, going back to the Panjab where they were cheapest. Later, he made money out of railway contracts and by planting rubber. He lived in Serendah in Selangor State for some time, and, according to the District Magistrate, exerted a great influence over the Sikh community there. He was also remembered as a litigious man, frequently seen in the law courts.[1]

He was living in Singapore in December 1913 when he came to Hong Kong with a suit against a partner, Mool Singh, who, he said, had run off with $1,200. He stayed at the *gurdwara* in Hong Kong and conducted his business from an office there. On 3 January, the birthday of Guru Gobind Singh, the tenth and last Sikh Guru, he spoke in the *gurdwara* and warmly espoused the cause of the *Ghadr* which was circulating through the Sikh colony. 'The main purpose of every Sikh', he said, 'was to fight for independence because Guru Gobind Singh died for his country.'[2] These were sentiments that had grown in him during his years in Malaya. There was a story that he sometimes told about travelling back to the Panjab with a very spiritual man from his village, returning by way of Madras and visiting temples as they went. In Hyderabad, on the way to the shrine of Hazur Sahib and the place where Guru Gobind Singh was slain, they were mocked by some Mahrattas who referred to the part played by the Sikhs in the Mutiny of 1857. Gurdit Singh replied that the people who helped the British were princes and kings, not the Sikhs, an answer that satisfied the Mahrattas but not himself; at that moment he felt that the Sikhs would have to prove their patriotism so they could walk with pride.

He could not stay at the *gurdwara* without being aware that there were several hundred men hanging about, desperately looking for a ship to Canada—illiterate, helpless men who had been up to two years in the Far East, unemployed or taking what work they could, and unwilling—having mortgaged family property—to go home until they had a chance to earn good money. A number approached Gurdit Singh after he spoke. A young Indian without means, Behari Lal Varma, had tried and failed to organize a company to charter a boat for Vancouver.[3] These men asked Gurdit Singh to do what he could to help. He saw it as an act of patriotism which, win or lose, would win him recognition among nationalists in India; and, before he left for Singapore, he promised, however difficult it was, to get a ship on his own.

Two students on their way to the United States, having broken their voyage at Hong Kong, were drawn into the project. They were Bir Singh from Tarn Taran in the Amritsar District and Daljit Singh from Muktesar in Ferozepore. Daljit Singh, who had been associate editor of a Sikh paper, *Khalsa Advocate*, in Amritsar, became Gurdit Singh's personal secretary and Bir Singh became his assistant secretary. They organized a passengers' committee and, on Gurdit Singh's instructions, began corresponding with the Khalsa Diwan Society in Vancouver.

The Prime Minister of Canada had to prod his officials before they tidied up the orders in-council that Chief Justice Hunter found faulty.[4] The new orders, P.C. 23 and 24, were issued on

7 January and Gurdit Singh knew about them by mid-February when he was in Calcutta looking for a ship.[5] But he only knew what he learned from the people in Vancouver and they were urging him to carry on, giving him every reason to believe that the Canadian law could be beaten. And something else was working inside him; something had triggered off a sense of mission and he was not really prepared to listen to pessimistic talk.

On 13 February, Gurdit Singh put out a prospectus announcing that he would charter a Chinese boat from Calcutta to Vancouver by way of Penang, Singapore, Hong Kong, and Shanghai. 'Our leaders living in America are requested to inform us by cabling the single letter "A" that we can land in North America with their assistance. On receipt of this cable we will sail for North America in our hired ship. If this cannot be arranged they should cable the letter "B", and we will pass on to Brazil. If this is impossible, they should cable us "C", in which case we will not sail at all.'[6] The committee at the *gurdwara* in Hong Kong wanted the ship to start at Hong Kong and they wired Gurdit Singh on 29 January. Although he did not come around to their point of view right away, he was forced to because he could not find a shipping company in Calcutta that would do business with him.

He came back to Singapore and got in touch with the assistant manager of the Straits Steam Ship Co., a Chinese he knew well. This man sent him to a shipping agent, Litho and Co., and he was shown two ships, S.S. *Hong Moh* and S.S. *Hong Bee*, which did not cost very much.[7] But when he asked around, he was told that they were very old and unfit for a Pacific crossing. A couple of days later he found another ship in good condition and priced low, but a friend warned him it would burn too much coal. All the while he was receiving impatient messages from Daljit Singh who was trying to raise money and having problems because everyone wanted to see the ship first. In the end, he settled his affairs in Singapore, and returned to Hong Kong, bringing his only child, seven-year-old Balwant Singh, with him. His childless first wife was no longer living, nor was his younger second wife who had died when Balwant was four months old.

An English firm, Jordan Co., was going to let him have a ship called *Kut Sang* at $9,000 a month, but backed out when he came around to sign the papers. He was certain that the British government was responsible for this. Then he met a German shipping agent, A. Bune, who offered him a small steamer which was being used to carry coal. This vessel, the *Komagata Maru*, had been built in Glasgow in 1890 for a German company, Dampfschiff Rederei Hansa of Hamburg, who registered her under the name *Stubbenhuk*. Until recently she had sailed as the *Sicilia* for the Hamburg Amerika Linie. Now she was owned by the Shinyei Kisen Goshi Kaisa, a Japanese company consisting of only four or five individuals and possessing only one other, smaller ship. She was about 100 metres long, 13 metres across and was driven by a 265 horsepower steam engine. There were a few cabins in the housing on her upper deck and there was a deck below which was as dirty as one might expect from her cargo.

The terms were six months at $11,000 Hong Kong per month: the first month to be paid on signing; the second within a week; the third and fourth within two weeks; and the remainder within two months of the commencement of the charter. The owners would provide the captain and the crew, but would not equip the ship with wireless telegraphy.[8]

Although Gurdit Singh told everyone that he was putting money of his own into the venture—and he may have—he intended to get most of what he needed from his passengers. Daljit Singh had been selling tickets at $210 Hong Kong which was equivalent to a return fare by a regular line. He had raised some $10,000 before any arrangements were made for a boat, and someone reported this to the Hong Kong police. They came to the *gurdwara* on the afternoon of 25 March, raided Gurdit Singh's office, and seized his papers. As it happened, he had signed a charter contract the day before, and, although the police brought him before a magistrate, they decided that they did not have a case against him. The incident worried a good many timid souls who did not like trouble with the authorities, and they backed out. Gurdit Singh, who had room for over 500 passengers, was left with only 165.[9]

He took over the *Komagata Maru* on 25 March. At his expense the lower deck was cleaned, fixed up with latrines, and furnished with 533 wooden benches, something like third class railway seats without backs. Aside from a barrel-shaped, portable coal stove, there were no other installations: no tables or chairs, simply the benches, spaced every one and a half metres, on which the passengers were to throw their bedding.[10] They went in quickly.

Gurdit Singh hired a Panjabi doctor and a *granthi* or priest, cleared the ship with the health officer, and announced that the *Komagata Maru* would sail at 10.00 a.m., Saturday, 28 March.

F. W. May, the Governor of Hong Kong, spotted trouble and cabled London while holding the ship, first by delaying the survey for her passenger certificate, and then by refusing to sign the certificate. On Monday, 30 March, on instructions from London, he cabled the Canadian government: '150 Indian Sikhs have chartered steamer from here to British Columbia, are not on through ticket from India. Am advised that local emigration clauses do not apply to other than Chinese emigration. Please telegraph whether in the circumstances they will be permitted to land in Canada.' Three days later, not receiving an answer, he sent a second, more urgent message. In the meantime, Gurdit Singh had gone to a firm of Hong Kong lawyers and they were pointing out—as the Governor knew very well—that he could not legally withhold his signature. On Saturday, 4 April, still with no word from Canada, he said the ship could go.

Gurdit Singh got the news from Claud Severn, the Colonial Secretary, a man he had known as a district magistrate in Selangor State fifteen years earlier. They had met by chance the day before: Gurdit Singh standing by the roadside in conversation with friends, Severn hailing him from a rickshaw. 'I did not know you were holding such a big position now,' Gurdit Singh said, 'otherwise I would have come to see you earlier.' He went around to Severn's office on the 4th, his pretext a social visit. He had presents which Severn refused to take, but he was received in a warm and friendly way. 'You are at liberty to embark', Severn said at once, explaining exactly what had happened. They spoke in Malay which Gurdit Singh could manage more easily than English. Severn wanted to know what the Sikh hoped to accomplish and Gurdit Singh said that his only desire was to help his fellow countrymen and co-religionists; he had no political purpose. In his announcements, Gurdit Singh had promised to fight in the Supreme Court of Canada 'for the decision in our favour for ever', and to go on to schedule further voyages. He spoke of these things to Severn, and said he would have four regular steamers operating between Calcutta and Vancouver and Bombay and Brazil and that 25,000 men were waiting for the service. 'What would you do if the Canadians do not allow you to land?' Severn asked, and Gurdit Singh answered that he did not think they could be kept out of Canada legally, but, if they were, they would go on to Brazil, a free and independent country and a good place for Indians to do business.[11]

Once he knew he could go, Gurdit Singh went straight to the *gurdwara* and told his people to get started. They held a prayer meeting, named their ship the *Guru Nanak Jahaz* after the first Sikh Guru, and trooped down to the port carrying their holy book, the *Granth Sahib*, with them. In his letter to Gurdit Singh's lawyers, Severn had stated quite clearly that permission to leave Hong Kong did not mean permission to land in Canada. Gurdit Singh knew that, but to make sure that his passengers did, the Hong Kong police came down to the boat with a printed piece of paper, the most recent notification of Canadian immigration regulations they could find. It was dated 9 April 1908, and did not impress anyone.[12] After all, Gurdit Singh had just been to see the Colonial Secretary and had been told that he could leave. The *Komagata Maru* cast off that evening with a large gathering on the shore to see her go. Her lights soon disappeared in the dark, the hymns of her passengers fading in the distance.

On Monday, the Governor advised Canada that the ship was on its way. On Tuesday came an answer to his two previous cables. The Canadian government were sorry they had not been able to reply earlier; entry would be prohibited.

In Ottawa, high officials were running for cover. The cables from Hong Kong had passed from the Governor-General's office, to External Affairs to the Department of the Interior, to be referred to the Immigration Branch, with no one sensing that this was something that had to be attended to immediately. It was not until Monday, 6 April, when it was already too late, that anyone picked up a phone to get action. From the Immigration Branch came the lame excuse that the order of 8 December—only one of the three orders that applied—had expired, and they had waited to find out if it had been renewed. The Prime Minister wanted explanations from everyone: the day and hour of every inter-departmental letter or phone call.[13]

On the morning of Wednesday, 8 April, the *Komagata Maru* reached Shanghai and anchored in the river at the outlet of the Yangtszepoo Creek. Bir Singh was already there, having gone ahead to recruit more passengers. Another member of the passen-

gers' committee, Harnam Singh of Khabra in the Lahore District,
had taken a steamer to Manila, and he and the people he rounded
up were to catch up with the *Komagata Maru* at Moji, Japan.
The second instalment of the charter was overdue; the third was
coming up and Gurdit Singh could not meet them unless he
collected another 100 fares.

An American reporter for the *China Press* came aboard after
three days and, interrupting Gurdit Singh's afternoon nap, gained
an interview. He was told that the voyage had been undertaken
to test the justice of the British towards all their people. 'If we are
admitted,' said Gurdit Singh, 'we will know that the Canadian
government is just. If we are deported we will sue the government and if we cannot obtain redress we will go back and take
up the matter with the Indian Government.'

'And what then?' the reporter asked.

'I cannot answer,' Gurdit Singh said with a broad smile, and his
companions, clustered around, laughed.[14]

The *Komagata Maru* was supposed to leave Shanghai on 10
April, two days after arrival, but waited because she did not have
as many paying passengers as she needed. Gurdit Singh, Daljit
Singh and Bir Singh talked boldly to put heart into those who
hesitated. 'They stopped us in Hong Kong,' Daljit Singh said.
'The Governor of Hong Kong would not let us go until he had
cabled the Governor-General of Canada. The Governor-General
of Canada communicated then with the Imperial Government
and word came back to let us go.'[15] Why had the British backed
down? Because they were afraid that the Sikh troops in Hong
Kong would revolt. What would happen if the ship was turned
back at Vancouver? There would be a revolution in India.

'I am leaving on the old man's ship,' Nanak Singh of Rawalpindi wrote from Shanghai to a friend in Vancouver, and he was
on his way on 15 April, one of 73 men from Shanghai along with
the 165 from Hong Kong.[16] Thirty-eight more, who still had to
raise their fares, were going to follow to board at Moji and Daljit
Singh had stayed behind to organize their departure. In London,
an account of the ship was picked up from German papers which
carried a German cable company item from Shanghai. It was
relayed to the Montreal *Star* and the Vancouver *Daily Province*
and a journalist ran around to Malcolm Reid to get a comment.
'The truth is', Reid said, 'we have had these rumours cropping

up so many times for the past year that we pay very little attention to them.'

On Sunday, 19 April, the *Komagata Maru* stopped at Moji, a coal and timber port 210 kilometres from Nagasaki on the island of Kyushu. Harnam Singh and eighty-five Sikhs he had collected in Manila were waiting in Nagasaki and they came on to Moji by train that day. In Moji, Gurdit Singh advertised for 2,000 tonnes of coal, enough to carry him to Vancouver and back—no more than he needed because, while it took 26 tonnes a day to fuel the *Komagata Maru*, she rode so lightly in the water that some cargo was necessary to steady her. A number of firms made offers, but all wanted money in advance, and he was able to pay for only 1,000 tonnes delivered on 21 April. The next instalment on the charter—$22,000 Hong Kong—was due, and under pressure from the owners, he told his agents to pay $17,000, promising the balance by 28 April.[17]

An appeal to the passengers produced $10,000 Hong Kong—$25 or $30 from each man in exchange for a receipt promising repayment in Vancouver. The Khalsa Diwan in Vancouver would make good, Gurdit Singh said, and if they did not, he would. On the 28th he was able to pay $2,500 in cash for more coal and $4,000 of the $5,000 owing to the owners. At this point, one of the owners offered a helping hand. Messrs Furukawa of Moji, who had sold Gurdit Singh his first 1,000 tonnes of coal, were prepared to sell him another 1,500 at 7 yen or $7.70 a tonne. (He had paid $10 a tonne for 350 tonnes in Hong Kong.) Gurdit Singh was 8,000 yen short, and Mr Akira Nagata of Shinysi Kisen Kaisa guaranteed payment and took a lien against the coal. He did this even though he understood that the *Komagata Maru* might be turned back at Vancouver.

The passengers spent these days sightseeing, viewing with perplexity the behaviour of the Japanese, especially the women who enjoyed a liberty never seen in a Panjabi village. It was a great surprise to see women in charge in shops and hotels, talking to strangers and laughing with them as if they knew them. Some young Indians stood outside a communal bath, tempted, but not daring to go in naked themselves. They wanted to keep on their underwear, but were refused with a smile by one of the ladies in attendance. One of Gurdit Singh's friends accosted the middle-aged manager of a restaurant where they had gone for a cup of tea: 'Why is there so much openness between the sexes?' But the answer did not satisfy. As far as Gurdit Singh was concerned, the Japanese islands were all centres of immorality. His companions probably agreed, even though several of them had found their way to the Yoshiwara, the red-light district, where a number picked up venereal infections during the week they were in Moji.[18]

Gurdit Singh was entertained at a hotel in Shimonoseki, across the straits from Moji, by Shinyei Kisen Kaisa's agent, Y. Sato, and some other Japanese gentlemen. The hotel was chosen 'for certain historical associations' (it was here that the Chinese and Japanese had signed treaties following the 1905 war with Russia); and there were speeches as well as dinner and geisha girls. Gurdit Singh's hosts said that they hoped India would wake up and be free because the Japanese would help; Japan, India, and China would in combination be strong enough to vanquish the countries of Europe. Gurdit Singh responded in kind. The Indian government, he boasted, had been threatened with a revolution led by ten thousand Indian troops if it continued to oppose the sailing of the *Komagata Maru*.[19]

At Shanghai and Moji, Gurdit Singh and his lieutenants had brought aboard bundles of the *Ghadr* and other revolutionary literature. Whenever passengers were gathered together, poems from the *Ghadr* or from a revolutionary anthology, *Ghadr di Gunj*, were read, recited, explained, paraphrased, and elaborated upon. The British were vilified, and the day of revolution promised. For men who had come more or less directly from their villages, all this was new and, perhaps, difficult to digest. But for those who had been in the Far East for a year or more, these were things they had heard before and they were ready to listen.

In Moji, Balwant Singh of Khurdpura came aboard to lecture twice. Balwant Singh, a big handsome man in his early thirties, was the priest at the *gurdwara* in Vancouver—the same priest who, with Bhag Singh, had managed to stir things up when he brought his family to Canada in 1912. In March 1913, he and two other delegates had gone to England to publicize the plight of their countrymen in Canada. They had gone on to India by way of Paris and Marseilles and, during the summer and autumn of 1913, they had held meetings throughout the Panjab, becoming increasingly bold in their attacks on the Canadian and Indian governments. At a big and excited meeting at Bradlaugh Hall in Lahore, Balwant Singh had cited a parable: the way to deal with a snake coiled round you is to rub its head against thorns. From the Governor of the Panjab himself had come a warning to stop this talk or face the consequences. Balwant Singh and his fellow delegates had asked for an interview and the Governor, Sir Michael O'Dwyer, had granted one. They asked to see the Viceroy, Lord Hardinge of Penshurst, and were sent on to him as well. They had made a great stir and now Balwant Singh was on his way back to Canada. He had arrived at Hong Kong a few days after the *Komagata Maru* left, but had overtaken her at Moji.[20]

While the *Komagata Maru* carried on around the islands to Yokohama, Gurdit Singh and Balwant Singh took a train to Kobe, the home of the Shinyei Kisen Kaisa, where Gurdit Singh signed an agreement extending the due date on the final instalment of the charter money from 28 May to 11 June.[21] The change was necessary because the voyage was now more than a week behind schedule. From Kobe the two went on to Yokohama where the *Komagata Maru* was waiting. Balwant Singh was taking an Osaka Shosen Kaisa liner to Victoria, and he urged Gurdit Singh to come with him, to make a fast crossing so that he could be in Canada before the *Komagata Maru*, but the passengers would not agree, and Gurdit Singh stayed on with them.

A few men arriving in Hong Kong after the *Komagata Maru* had left, had cabled ahead to ask her to wait. In a party of 14, they boarded at Yokohama, and they brought the passenger total to 376: 24 Muslims, 12 Hindus, and 340 Sikhs.[22] The Muslims were from Shahpur in the western Punjab. There was the odd Sikh from the high plateau country of Rawalpindi or the sub-montane district of Ambala—from the dry region of Hissar or the hill country of Sialkot. But most of the passengers came from villages in the fertile central Panjab plain: from the districts of Amritsar, Patiala, Ferozepore, Ludhiana, Jullunder, and Lahore, the heart of the Sikh homeland, the most densely populated part of the Panjab. The largest contingent came from the monotonously flat country of Amritsar, Gurdit Singh's own district, where excessive irrigation and bad drainage had been driving people off their land for the past ten years.

All but fifteen were bedded down on the lower deck, sharing a common kitchen. Gurdit Singh and his small son had a cabin. So did the ship's young medical officer, Dr Rughunath Singh, on leave from the 8th Rajputs in Hong Kong and travelling with his wife and one child. One other passenger, Sundar Singh of Timonwal, Amritsar, had his wife, a son, and a baby daughter with him and he was also given a cabin. The remaining cabin space went to those who had taken a lead in organizing the voyage: Daljit Singh, Bir Singh, Harnam Singh of Khabra, Amir Mohammed Khan of Ludhiana. These men paid nothing extra and it was the nature of this ship that no one complained.[23].

Bhagwan Singh Jakh, who had left Victoria in handcuffs, a prisoner on the *Empress of Japan*, had jumped ship in Yokohama and he was still there, five months later, planning his return to North America. He was staying with Maulvi Barkatullah, a militant pan-Islamist from Bhopal State who had just been stripped of a professorship in Hindustani at the University of Tokyo. The two of them visited the *Komagata Maru*, bringing the latest copies of the *Ghadr* with them, and Bhagwan Singh gave a fiery address. But he had some discouraging words for Gurdit Singh. You will not get permission to land, he said; the Canadian government will make sure of that.

If Gurdit Singh had not been sure of himself and the will of God, he would not have come as far as he had. 'This journey is absolutely according to the terms of the Canadian government,' he said, 'so no power on earth can stop us in Vancouver.'[24]

4

ARRIVAL

The Canadian authorities were alerted and waiting, having been informed by British consular officers in Japan of the steamer's progress from Moji to Yokohama and of her departure for Victoria on Saturday, 2 May. They knew Gurdit Singh's name, although not much else about him, and they had seen and translated one of his advertisements or placards which an informant, cultivated by Hopkinson, had taken from the *gurdwara* in Vancouver. Two days after the *Komagata Maru* left Yokohama, Malcolm Reid filed a wireless message asking for her expected time of arrival. The message was to be relayed by the *Empress of India*, then five days out from Vancouver, but the *Komagata Maru*, carrying no wireless, approached in silence.

Balwant Singh stepped off his steamer at Victoria on 20 May, spoke to a meeting of Sikhs at the Victoria *gurdwara* and then came on to Vancouver. Late in the afternoon of the same day, Husain Rahim and Rajah Singh, secretary of the United India League in Vancouver, a well-built, six-foot veteran of the Imperial Service Corps, hired a forty-foot, sea-going launch out of Port Alberni. Their lawyer, Bird, had spotted an error in the order-in-council prohibiting the landing of labourers: of all the ports in British Columbia, Port Alberni was the only one not mentioned so it was obviously the place for the *Komagata Maru* to berth. But she had to be told. Port Alberni sits at the head of a long inlet from the Pacific, and Rahim and Rajah Singh made the run in seven or eight hours, arriving at Pachina Bay on the remote and wild south-western shore of Vancouver Island at 8 a.m. on the 21st. During the morning and early afternoon they battled heavy seas until, at 2 p.m., they gave up and headed back to the Bamfield Creek cable station near the entrance to the Alberni inlet. They had intended to go on to a sheltered bay to watch the traffic in the strait, but it had been too rough. The next morning they were going to try again, sitting five to eight kilometres off shore in the main shipping lane, but, in the meantime, the *Komagata Maru* ploughed by.[1]

The immigration people tipped off the moment Rahim took out a launch, sent H. L. Good, the nearest customs inspector, in pursuit and made haste to get there themselves. Good caught up with the two Indians at Bamfield Creek and did what he could to sabotage their efforts, getting the government telegraph operator to refuse them use of the telephone, and arranging, with a $25 bribe, to foul the mechanism of their motor launch. That evening, Reid, Hopkinson, and assistant Hindi interpreter Henry Gwyther, crossed from the mainland to Nanaimo, eighty to ninety-five kilometres from Port Alberni, only to learn that the *Komagata Maru* had arrived at the William's Head quarantine station near Victoria. Like men possessed, they drove through the night—about one hundred and twenty kilometres of rough and dangerous road in a rented Ford with a driver not too sure of his way—leaving Nanaimo at 10.30 at night, stopping at the Dominion Hotel in Victoria at 3.30 in the morning, and then, an hour and a half later, on their way again, pulling up at the outer wharf at William's Head at 6.30 a.m.[2]

There they saw the *Komagata Maru* riding at anchor against a backdrop of mountain peaks. Her passengers were on deck, squatting in groups as they prepared their morning meal. As the government launch came out, they lined the bulwarks, fore and aft: Muslims in red caps and Sikhs, both bearded and clean-shaven, in turbans of many different colours—most of the men wearing European three-button jackets, some in white shirts and ties, and a few in khaki uniforms from past military service. A large launch with a number of local Indians approached and circled the steamer, trying to get past an immigration patrol boat. The Reverend L. W. Hall of the Hindu Friend Society of Victoria was there and he tackled the officials on behalf of the whole group, pleading for permission to speak to those on board; but, although he was not easily put off, he and his party eventually gave up and went back to Victoria.

The quarantine officer—who found the passengers and the ship in good shape after a fair weather crossing—had not finished his examination, and when Reid and Hopkinson discovered that the

Komagata Maru was chartered through to Vancouver, they left without going on board. For a few hours it seemed that the ship might be turned back by the quarantine officer because, while the clearance papers from Hong Kong, Shanghai, and Yokohama were in order, the cheery little captain, T. Yamamoto, did not have a bill of health from Moji. But Daljit Singh turned up a certificate of fumigation and at 6.45 in the afternoon the ship was given her pratique. She sailed that evening for Vancouver, her medical officer, Dr Rughunath Singh under instructions to vaccinate every passenger while under way. Reid had wanted a patrol boat to go with her, but none was available and the *Komagata Maru* steamed into the night unaccompanied but with three immigration officers aboard. As she passed a lighthouse on an American island about thirty kilometres from Victoria, a Japanese crewman, Nakajima Hirosuke, 29 years of age, jumped and tried to swim for shore, but the currents were very strong and Captain Yamamoto judged that he did not make it.

In the early hours of Saturday, 23 May, the *Komagata Maru* anchored on the far side of the Burrard Inlet, opposite Vancouver. At dawn the passengers were out on deck with tree-covered mountains rising behind them and the city across the water in front. They were dressed in their best with their bags packed, ready to go ashore. At 8 a.m. a launch came out with customs officials, a medical inspector, the shipping agent to whom the *Komagata Maru* had been consigned, and a party of immigration inspectors, Hopkinson and Reid at their head. Gurdit Singh had heard of these men from Bhagwan Singh. In Hopkinson he saw a lean, swarthy, six-foot two-inch man of thirty-four with, as Rahim described him, a half-eastern, half-western air. (By his own colleagues Hopkinson was taken for a half-caste, although, if they had asked him, he would have said he was English.)[3] Reid was also a tall man, three or four years older than Hopkinson, pallid in complexion, with a full moustache waxed at the ends, and now, as he stood on the deck, very tight and unbending in his manner.

Gurdit Singh had already spoken to the press who had come alongside in launches at William's Head. 'We are British citizens and we consider we have a right to visit any part of the Empire', he said. 'We are determined to make this a test case and if we are refused entrance into your country, the matter will not end here.' He spoke in this vein to Hopkinson. 'What is done with this shipload of my people will determine whether we shall have peace in all parts of the British Empire.'[4]

Late in the morning the ship was moved over towards the Vancouver side of the inlet, and the passengers thought they were going ashore, but the anchor was dropped about a kilometre out, in front of the immigration building at the foot of Burrard Street. Gathered on the waterfront were the Sikhs from Vancouver; and, when the *Komagata Maru* came closer, one of them began signalling by semaphore, at last drawing the attention of a signaller on the ship and wigwagging a few brief messages before he was chased off by the C.P.R. police. Some of the press came out to talk to Captain Yamamoto and the passengers who happily posed for pictures, but after they left, no one else was allowed to come close.

Acting for Y. Sato and Co., agents for the owners of the *Komagata Maru*, was C. Gardner Johnson, a local shipping broker who had long done business with Japanese shipping companies. It was his job to collect $15,000 in gold for the balance of the charter money and for the coal taken on at Moji. This had to be paid by 11 June or the owner would have the right to take the ship back to Hong Kong whether or not the passengers had landed. Reid knew it because Gardner Johnson obligingly told him, and he decided to do everything he could to make sure the charter money was not paid and then to drag his feet and wait for 11 June. He told his superiors in Ottawa what he was doing and no complaint came back.[5]

'You know I am a merchant and there is no law to prevent merchants from going on shore', Gurdit Singh said. 'You can detain the passengers, not me; you are responsible for the damages.'[6] He might as well have spoken to a deaf man; and, for that matter, Reid made every effort to be deaf, staying away from the ship after the first day and keeping the press away as well. After a couple of days Gurdit Singh had that as a complaint too. He wanted the press on board; he wanted to see a representative from every Vancouver daily newspaper. But the only people he saw were Reid's subordinates and Gardner Johnson who periodically made demands for payment. An immigration launch with armed guards (taken from the waiting list for the police force and paid $4.00 a shift) circled the ship day and night. And Gurdit Singh stayed a prisoner, unable to go to the banks or to make contact with the local Indians.

The immigration agent, making a show of processing the men on board, sought every excuse for delay. His medical officer spent three days finding seventy-seven cases of trachoma, a chronic inflammation of the eye, very difficult to cure, and a standard ground for disqualification. Full physical examinations occupied several more days. To be sure, a thorough examination of close to 400 people must be a time-consuming affair, but for Canadian immigration at that time it was unusual. Even though the first and only examination was at the port of entry, it was ordinarily a very brisk affair: the medical officer touched the forehead to see if it was hot, mumbled a question to catch the deaf or dumb, and, if the immigrant had a healthy complexion and a normal appearance, looked no further. An Englishman had only to identify himself as a British citizen and he was whisked through with a quick inspection of his scalp for ringworm. The examination was always a bit more careful for those who did not come from Britain or Northern Europe. But it was still so cursory that, at the port of Quebec, two doctors, working at a normal rate, could pass 300 immigrants in an hour. If called upon to go faster, they could clear 400 or 500 in an hour, pushing people through at the rate of eight or nine a minute.[7]

J. Edward Bird, hired and instructed by Rahim and a committee of fifteen local Indians, announced that he was representing all 376 passengers. He wanted to see his clients but was barred from the ship. The immigration officials would carry letters—which were no substitute for an interview—but they did not want a lawyer running back and forth between the Sikhs on shore and those on the boat. 'Gurdit Singh', Bird complained, 'is even more a prisoner than if he were in a penitentiary.'[8] He appealed to Ottawa, and was told he would have to accept whatever arrangement the immigration agent judged appropriate.

On the fifth day, Bird saw the lawyers on the other side, Robie L. Reid, a senior partner in a local law firm which looked after most government legal work in Vancouver, and W. B. A. Ritchie, the Immigration Department's chief legal counsel—once the Prime Minister's law partner, and still his personal friend. Bird wanted to speed things up. They wanted to make sure—remembering what had happened with the *Panama Maru*—that, if a case went to court, it went to the highest court in the province. It seemed to them that Bird had too many strings to his bow. If he was refused a writ of *habeas corpus*, he could go from one justice to another, but, under the law of British Columbia, the case was closed and the government had no appeal if a writ was ever issued.

They told him he could have two or three test cases right away if he agreed to take them straight to the Court of Appeal. (He could accomplish this by allowing a case to be dismissed without argument in a lower court.) Then the issue would be decided by a full panel instead of a single—perhaps maverick— judge. It was a better offer than the immigration agent would have supported, and coming from Ritchie, it was bound to be endorsed by the bureaucrats in Ottawa. Behind it, unspoken, was the threat that, if Bird did not agree, he could wait till Kingdom Come before he had a chance to plead his case.[9]

Bird agreed—after two hours of fierce bargaining—but he had to go back to Rahim and his people and they said 'no'. They would make no deals; they would abandon no options; they were going to fight through the courts every inch of the way, regardless of time or money.

At the end of the week, they held a great meeting in a hired hall, drawing 500 or 600 Indians and about 20 whites—a couple of reporters and Hopkinson and his stenographer among them. Rahim was in the chair and Balwant Singh, speaking in Panjabi, gave the principal address. Even with Hopkinson there, he was pretty daring. A man who had used some striking similes in Lahore was not going to be too careful in Vancouver. He spoke of a changing mood in India, a return to the spirit of 1857, a new unity against the English, and the inevitability of revolution if Indians did not get home rule within the next few years. He talked about the exclusion laws in the white dominions and of the weakness of the Indian government within the Empire. Then, finishing with a reference to Sikh warriors of the past who fought three times against the English, he called on his audience for funds for the *Komagata Maru*.[10]

A lot of men wanted to speak when Balwant Singh sat down, but Rahim cut them off. This meeting was called for business, he said, not talk. What was needed was hard cash: enough to keep the ship in Vancouver however Reid tried to delay. The hall was full of men who never banked but carried savings in their pockets or turbans, and, as this money spilled out, a pile of five, ten, and even one hundred dollar-bills rose on a table in front of the speakers. The largest contribution was $2,000. When the contributions slackened, another speaker, Bhag Singh or some other member of the committee, would rise to stoke the fire of religious and patriotic fervour, and, as the meeting ended, $5,000 in cash lay on the table with another $66,000 in pledges.

On Monday, 1 June, the medical inspection at last complete, Malcolm Reid began ferrying passengers back and forth, one at a time, for Board of Inquiry hearings in his office. Instead of taking the first man on the list, a typical passenger who would have made a good test case, he started with twenty men who had been in Canada before, landing thirteen more or less automatically, and then making an issue of the rest, spending two days on two cases that were worth no more than five minutes each. The proceedings were a joke, Bird told the press, who were not sympathetic but whom he used effectively. 'We want the officials to examine a man who has never been in Canada before. I wanted them to take the case of Gurdit Singh, but this case they specifically stated they would take last.'[11]

The Indians on shore told Bird to boycott the hearings which he did for a day. Then, on Thursday, 4 June, when an immigration inspector came out for the remaining Indians who had been resident in Canada, Gurdit Singh refused to let them go, announcing that he and his fellow passengers had resolved to die starving to protest against the treatment they were receiving.

Later that day, Gurdit Singh was taken on one launch and Bird brought alongside on another, and, with immigration officials plastered around them, listening to every word, they met for the first time. Bird had been unhappy about these arrangements, but, after making a fuss, had accepted them as better than nothing. They talked for an hour, and Gurdit Singh had bitter words for the leaders of the local community who had encouraged him to come. What came out of this meeting was a proposal that Gurdit Singh provide a proper detention shed so he could free his ship, unload his coal, take on new cargo—presumably timber—and send the *Komagata Maru* back to Hong Kong. If the passengers were ordered deported, he would find another ship to send them back, and he would pay their keep until then. In the meantime, he would leave for India on the *Empress of Russia* sailing on 11 June.

'I strongly oppose', Reid told Ottawa, afraid that the Indians would take it as a sign of weakness, warning that the move could provoke white riots.[12] It would be difficult, dangerous, and expensive to guard such a large body of men for a long time; there was no suitable building; and, he said, turning from excuses to his real motive, there was every chance that by holding firm and waiting for Gurdit Singh to default, the government could be rid of the whole problem in a week.

There was no reason under Canadian law for keeping Gurdit Singh when he wanted to take the next boat back. But Reid argued that the old man, given the chance, would agitate and create trouble for the Indian government and so put pressure on Canada. So Gurdit Singh was to stay where he was.

The danger of riot was something that Reid talked about more than anyone else. It was true that bodies like the city council and the Board of Trade had called on the government to use every possible means to keep the *Komagata Maru* men out. Vancouver, a raw, new city that had grown tremendously in the previous ten or twelve years, was now in the midst of a slump with some building trades reporting sixty per cent of their men out of work. The situation was tricky. In the early spring, white labour in British Columbia had been demanding the few jobs held by Indians and two timber companies had given way, laying off quite a number to replace them with other men. But there had been no organized demonstrations, no incidents in which matters threatened to get out of hand. In any case, Reid was laying hands on an argument rather than expressing a genuine concern.

For two days, Gurdit Singh had been telling officials that his people had very little to eat, insisting that the immigration department feed them since he could not go ashore himself. Reid was unimpressed, although he sent out 200 tonnes of water, enough for two or three weeks. When Gurdit Singh announced a hunger strike, Reid scoffed, apparently with justification because the Japanese crew soon reported that the passengers were cooking at night and that their leader was taking all his regular meals.[13] On Friday, 6 June, Gurdit Singh sent messages to the King and the Governor-General: 'No provisions since four days Reid refuses supply charterer and passengers starving kept prisoners.' When he gave them to an immigration officer—the only way he could send anything ashore—he handed over $40 for transmission and prepaid answers, which prompted Reid to say that if Gurdit Singh had $40 for cables, he had funds for food. A list of the groceries that the passengers wanted—100 bags of flour, ginger, cabbage, a quarter of a tonne of purified butter, 10 boxes of milk, 50 live sheep or goats, 200 boxes of cigarettes, red peppers, spices and crates of eggs—struck Reid as preposterous, and so the matter stood. Late that afternoon, Husain Rahim phoned to say that his committee had loaded five tonnes of food on a Japanese fishing boat and wished to take it out. Instead it was transferred to an immigration launch and carried out by the officials only to be waved off by Gurdit Singh standing at the rail.

By the end of the weekend, real hunger had taken the ship, although Gurdit Singh and the four or five close to him still had food in their kitchen which was separate from the common kitchen.[14] The old man was no democrat. The ship's doctor, Rughunath Singh, sent a note to shore saying that he and his wife and child had nothing to eat and that he was unable to give medical attention to all the people in his charge. On Monday afternoon, Hopkinson, by request, appeared on board to be met by Daljit Singh and led into the saloon where they waited for several minutes before Gurdit Singh and a couple of his henchmen joined them. His people, Gurdit Singh said, had gone on a hunger strike believing that the Canadians would take note. He now saw that they were quite unconcerned and that there was no fair dealing here, even from a humanitarian point of view. Hopkinson was able to strike a neutral pose, a reason why he was effective in his work. He did not give an inch, yet came away with a $10 gold piece and £18 sterling from the old man's purse. Arrangements were made with a wholesale grocery and at 8 that evening enough food was put on board to give all the passengers one good meal.

On Tuesday, 9 June, when Gurdit Singh let the rest of the Indians who had been in Canada go ashore, ending his boycott, Daljit Singh tried to jump into the immigration launch with them, insisting that Mr Reid had said they could send a steward into town for supplies. Hopkinson offered to let the doctor, Rughunath Singh, accompanied by an official, do the shopping instead. In that case, Gurdit Singh said, his people would do without.

The last five returning Canadians were landed that day, leaving 355 passengers behind. With no choice now but to examine new men, Reid started with the physically unfit, eighty-eight in all (seventy-seven with trachoma and eleven with other disabilities), because he could reject them without citing the orders-in-council that Bird was so anxious to test.

On the morning of the 10th, Hopkinson sensed an uneasy mood among the passengers. It was possible, he thought, that Gurdit Singh and those around him might receive some rough treatment if no food was forthcoming. But he was wrong. The old man was completely in control, deeply respected and trusted by all but two or three on board. So far the ship had been an orderly place, except for an incident on the evening of the 1st when a couple of passengers had grabbed a guard and force-walked him over to the gangway, and Reid had been warned to keep his men off at night. Reid, himself, was staying on shore, but his staff, coming and going during the day without mishap, thought him a great coward.

Captain Yamamoto had heard from Kobe and was to leave on the 11th if the $15,000 was not paid. Gardner Johnson and Sir Charles Hibbert Tupper—former cabinet minister and lifetime friend of the present Prime Minister and now acting as counsel for the owners—had promised to help in every way. From Reid's viewpoint the prognosis was good. The government might have to provision the ship when it went back, but he was not going to send anything out until the passengers had no choice but to leave.

5

DELAY

On the 10th, the last possible day, Rahim presented Gardner Johnson with a cheque for $11,000 which he said he would pay over if the charter was assigned to his committee. This offer was most unwelcome, and the shipping agent would not recommend it to the owners, although he had to tell them about it and wait for their answer. No one was quite sure what Rahim's game was. The officials half-hoped that he was bluffing or that Gurdit Singh would not relinquish the charter. On the 11th, Rahim's committee sent out several tonnes of food, and both sides waited for word from Kobe. That evening Reid adjourned the Board of Inquiry with the excuse that his staff needed to attend to their regular office work. He was waiting for Rahim's negotiations to collapse.

However, the owners were interested. If they sent the ship back they would get no income from it until it reached Hong Kong, and, more to the point, they were afraid that Gurdit Singh would sue. So they replied suggesting terms, and Gardner Johnson drew up a proposal which he was sure Rahim and his friends could not meet. They would be asked to put up the $15,000 due on the 11th, $1,600 for the installation of a wireless, $200 for provisions each day the ship was in port, $6,000 for provisions for the return voyage, legal expenses, which already amounted to $250, and $10,307 for two months hire from 1 June. The last was particularly unreasonable since Gurdit Singh had already paid the hire of the *Komagata Maru* for June and most of July, having defaulted only on the fifth and sixth months.

Rahim somehow kept discussions going. The weekend passed; Monday came and went; and the *Komagata Maru* remained at her moorings. Reid, highly excited, decided to ask the Japanese government to recall the boat, not thinking for a minute that if such an appeal was advisable, it should be made at a higher level.

He went to the Japanese consul in Vancouver, Y. A. Hori, who sent a cable to the Japanese Ministry of Foreign Affairs. It happened that two Japanese cruisers, the *Asama* and the *Azuma*, were due to visit Vancouver on the weekend and Reid—evidently —thought they could be used to intimidate the passengers and force the *Komagata Maru* back home. He was not a very sophisticated man. The press, picking it up, reported that Yamamoto was going to invite bluejackets aboard or get up steam and make a run for international water, or that the Canadian government might give him an escort until he was safely out of Canadian water and then hand him over to the Japanese.

On Tuesday the 16th, the harbour master asked Yamamoto to make room for the cruisers by shifting to a new berth about 275 metres up the inlet. The captain told his engineers to get up steam, and the passengers, suspicious and alarmed as soon as they heard what was afoot, rushed to the engine room, sticks in their hands, to stop them. Gardner Johnson went out to reason with them; Hopkinson argued with them an hour; but they did not believe that 275 metres would be the extent of the voyage. In the end, the harbour master decided to leave the *Komagata Maru* where she was.

Gurdit Singh said the passengers had acted on their own, and Hopkinson, believing him, thought he had lost control. In truth, the inspector had been talking to three men whom he took for a faction but who were really very isolated. They were the ship's doctor, Rughunath Singh, and two other passengers, Bhan Singh, a schoolmaster from Jullunder, and Pohlo Ram, his friend from Anandpur. The youthful Rughunath Singh had been allowed ashore for medicines and had talked at length with the officials, giving them a great catalogue of charges and complaints against Gurdit Singh, promising a full written report in Panjabi.[1] He saw his own case as quite separate from that of the other passengers and, although he was not the kind of man who looked for trouble, he had decided the best way to get himself and his family off the ship was to co-operate with the authorities. Solidarity on the ship was maintained at meetings held every evening. At one of these meetings Gurdit Singh denounced the doctor as a government detective and then posted four or five guards in front of his cabin and another five or six on top. After that Bhan Singh and Pohlo Ram found it wise to keep their own counsel.

By this time, the Board of Inquiry had met on eight occasions without ordering anyone deported. Reid was working very slowly through the medical cases and, at the end of each hearing, reserving judgment—making no decisions so there would be no decisions to challenge in court. The Act said any passenger detained by an immigration officer had to be examined 'forthwith' and 'immediately' landed or rejected. That was not happening, but the public did not care, and Reid felt himself impregnable. When counsel Bird threatened to get a writ to compel him to make a judgment, he said bluntly that he did not consider himself obliged to pay the slightest attention to any court orders, if any were made.[2]

All hinged on a word from Kobe. Gardner Johnson was doing what he could, telling the owners that the negotiations by the local Indians were not genuine, only designed to buy time, reminding them that delay meant greater loss, assuring them that their legal position was sound, and dismissing Gurdit Singh's threat to bring suit with the comment that it was unavoidable 'in any event'. On Thursday the 18th, they ordered the ship back if two months' hire was not paid within twenty-four hours. But they were worried about litigation and asked for an official statement that the passengers had been prevented from landing by regulation and not by their action. Reid had a letter drafted and then was warned by the lawyers Robie Reid and W. B. A. Ritchie that his words could be used against him. How could he say what the Board of Inquiry verdict would be before it was given? He decided to refer to Ottawa before he let it go.[3]

Time ran out on Reid, not the Indians. For forty-eight hours he campaigned frantically to preserve his independence of the courts, to prevent a reassignment of the charter, and to convince the owners that they could order the ship back with impunity. But he met defeat. As the *Asama* and *Azuma* steamed into Vancouver harbour on Saturday morning, 20 June, he was hiding from a bailiff while Rahim and Bhag Singh were delivering another $4,000 to Gardner Johnson. He was avoiding service of a writ while they were announcing themselves as the new charterers of the *Komagata Maru*. They had raised $18,000 in cash contributions large and small, $1,000 from their friends in California and the rest among their own people in British Columbia. While the transfer had not yet been approved by the owners and

Reid was doing everything he could to stop it, hard cash was a powerful argument and it had bought time for the men on the *Komagata Maru.*

Daljit Singh sent a note to Bhag Singh. 'We cannot fully thank you for your kindness which you have done us by paying the instalment. We hope you will try your best for the landing of the passengers in the same way. Now pray, do not waste money on lawyers in this way, but oblige him to try for an early landing for Baba Gurdit Singh Ji. Everything will be all right then. We will be in loss till Baba Ji is a prisoner in this way. So try for Baba Ji's landing with all your heart first of all. Do inform us of the activity of the lawyer in this respect.'4

But the men on shore had different priorities and they were calling the tune. Having sunk $15,000 into the venture, they asked themselves how much more it was going to cost with provisions, legal fees, port dues, and no end in sight. Three weeks previously they had refused to bargain with the other side. Now they backed down, and, on their instructions, Bird went around to the government lawyers and asked them to repeat the offer made on 27 May—to give him a test case without delay if he would go straight to the Court of Appeal. They invited him to make the offer himself and he did so in writing that morning, asking for a reply by the following Monday.5

The Khalsa Diwan Society and the United India League called a meeting at a downtown hall for the afternoon of Sunday, 21 June. Mitt Singh, secretary of the gurdwara committee, standing at a street corner with some of his countrymen, said, 'Let's tell the immigration people that we are going to hold a meeting on Sunday.' He was looking at Baboo Singh, one of Hopkinson's informants, one of the three men threatened with destruction after Bhagwan Singh had been deported. Someone else said, 'Baboo will tell them anyway.' And Baboo Singh, defiantly, said, 'Yes, I will tell them.'6

Four hundred Indians attended and 125 whites from the Socialist party. As usual, Hopkinson was there with his stenographer, and, as usual, Rahim was in the chair. Bird was the main speaker. His remarks, which ran on for more than half an hour, were addressed to the whites and he had his eye particularly on the immigration inspector.

'Now I am not here as a politician', he began, after the assembled Sikhs had chanted a hymn from the *Granth Sahib*. 'I am in this matter simply as a lawyer and I have tried to the best of my ability to get a test case before the courts for the purpose of finding out as to whether these men are entitled to land or not. They came here on the 22nd day of May and since that time I have been sparring for an opening to the best of my ability, trying to get a case before the Court to test the validity of the Act—the Immigration Act—and of the Orders-in-Council under that Act, and I have sparred in vain for an opening. I have not been able to get anything before the Court on any reasonable excuse whatever that would test the Orders-in-Council. Why I have not been able to do this, gentlemen, I cannot say. I can only surmise that the instructions from the Department at Ottawa to the Immigration authorities here was to delay matters and delay matters and procrastinate and delay until such time as these people were starved back to their original port from whence they sailed.'[7]

He spoke with feeling. 'They talk about socialists and anarchists. There is no set of anarchists in Canada like the Immigration Officials who defy all law and order. . . .' As he came to the end, he looked at Hopkinson: 'I can see some of the Immigration Officials right here—I say they can go back and say their plans are known . . .' and he issued a warning. His clients were not quitting. The tactics of the immigration department would not work. 'Do not blame the Hindus if you see this farce dragged on for months. If necessary they can wait a century—perhaps they will all die before this thing is decided.'

Rahim had invited two or three members of the Socialist party to speak and one of them, H. M. 'Fritz' Fitzgerald, made it to the platform, creating a sensation among the press who had never heard a white man preach to an audience of orientals as he did. Sohan Lal, Balwant Singh, Rajah Singh, and other members of the Shore Committee took over, in Panjabi, where he left off, bolder than ever, holding nothing back. Something would have to be done about them very shortly, Hopkinson wrote afterwards to the Deputy Minister; if there was a law that would apply to them, they should be deported; it would have a salutary effect on the whole community.

Malcolm Reid wanted to ignore Bird's writ or any other court action. It had to be done, he explained to Ottawa because the

Indians, in court, were liable to win. As a precaution, he had sent one member of his Board of Inquiry, Inspector Thomas Elliott, out of town on an invented mission, so the Board could not meet. So far Reid had been allowed his head. Now he was reined in. The immigration act required an immediate decision once a Board of Inquiry had completed its examination. That was how the Superintendent of Immigration, W. D. Scott, read it, and that is what he told Reid by wire that Sunday (21 June). If Reid's decisions were not taken in accordance with the act, they would be open to judicial examination; and, Scott warned him, he should be very careful about that. He was allowed some discretion, but he could not have a licence to trample over court orders. On one point he was directly countermanded: 'Elliott should be on hand.'[8] Sending him away was too obvious a ploy to delay proceedings.

Behind Reid, pushing hard, was the M.P., H. H. Stevens, only recently back in town following the parliamentary recess. As the immigration staff in Vancouver knew, he was the man making the decisions. In fact, the Immigration Office was run practically as an adjunct to his local Conservative association—all staff appointments made through the association executive, the back-up patrol boat, used in the 24-hour watch on the *Komagata Maru*, hired from an active party member, and Reid, when he took on six stout police candidates as special guards, obliged to defend himself for not picking party faithful.[9]

Harry Stevens was a first-term M.P., elected in the Conservative sweep of 1911 in a riding most people had conceded to the standing Liberal member. He was a head shorter than Reid, a couple of years younger, a man of little formal education but great resolution and energy. In this instance he was sure that his Eastern colleagues did not understand what was going on, a common British Columbian complaint. Some of his constituents said that the government was wobbling on the issue, not taking a tough stand, and, while he would not admit it publicly, that was his concern.

The day before (20 June) he had interviewed Rughunath Singh to get the facts for the Prime Minister, to put him straight about the situation on the ship. The poor doctor—who was certainly getting the worst of it at that time—was brought ashore and introduced to Stevens in the Immigration Office where a stenographer waited to take down everything he said.

'Some of them threatened you out there did they?' Stevens said without finesse, and Rughunath Singh said yes, Gurdit Singh had threatened him, and his men had said they would kill him if he went ashore or went near the gangway.[10] 'They think I have spoken against them.' In his story Gurdit Singh was a trickster and a tyrant who had sold the passengers a bill of goods and now held mastery over them through intimidation and misinformation. 'I have tried to make them understand but they are against me', he said. 'All the men practically believe in him though they know in their minds what he has done to them.'

Half-way through, disconcerted by the stenographer, he sought some assurance that the conversation would not be published. 'This is for myself and Mr Borden', Stevens told him.

At one point, Stevens asked for absolution of the immigration officials. 'What we want to know', he said to Rughunath Singh, 'is that you have been treated as fairly and as responsibly as we could treat you. I wanted to know that you are satisfied, and I think if the men on board really understood that they would be much more satisfied wouldn't they?' The doctor did not dare to disagree.

Towards the end, Stevens asked if the passengers would go away peaceably if provisions were put on board. The answer was no. 'They do not want to go back—they will try their best to land.'

With the government lawyers and Bird nearing agreement on a test case, Stevens did what he could to put pressure on the Prime Minister. On Wednesday, 24 June, Borden received a fistful of telegrams from British Columbia, including one from the Mayor of Vancouver reporting on a mass meeting the night before at which Stevens had been the star attraction.[11] One moment had rung in the ears long after the meeting was over—the resounding applause that followed Stevens' attack on the British Columbia judiciary. 'Some say "Why do you not go to the courts?" I say we are willing to go to the courts if we can find an honest court to go to.'[12]

To its credit, one Vancouver daily had criticized the calling of this meeting, and, if Stevens had really been concerned about the danger of bloodshed, he would have thought better of it too.[13] Happily, the crowd was orderly, if noisy. A party of Sikhs, turned back at the entrance, the hall already jammed, were jostled a bit. The socialist, Fitzgerald, had his hat bashed in. And Rahim, trying to speak from the balcony as the hall emptied, was hustled away by a police officer to the shouts and cheers of the crowd.

By Wednesday, the ship was short of water, and Reid, with the authority to supply it if necessary, chose to do nothing. The passengers consumed fourteen tonnes a day, eight to cook, drink, and wash, six for steam for the generator: $28 a day, not a great matter for a government which was going to have to pay thousands to send the ship back, but a weapon that Reid willingly used.

That day, Reid wired Ottawa: 'Legal advisers anxious to bring test case in courts. Stevens agrees with me in opposing this.' Stevens wanted to pack the passengers off on the *Empress* sailing at 11 a.m. the next day. He would bring the *Empress* alongside and use whatever force was necessary, putting guards on board for the voyage back. It would cost $15,000, paying a C.P.R. charity rate of $35 a head, and he and Reid would take care of all the details once they had permission to go ahead. As an argument, they conjured up the spectre of street riots if the issue dragged on any longer.

No one in Ottawa liked the plan, and the Prime Minister himself drafted a reply rejecting it. The risks were too great. More than that, Borden agreed with E. Blake Robertson, the Assistant Superintendent of Immigration, who saw no good in attempting to keep the Indians out of court 'by sharp practices'.[14] It was late in the day, but at last someone was showing some respect for the law.

On Thursday morning, 25 June, the government's lawyers bade Reid bring two men ashore so that Bird could choose one and go straight ahead with a test case. They were Munshi Singh of Hoshiarpur and Narain Singh of Lahore, and Bird had picked them from the passenger list because they had only a small amount of money and would be representative of the rest.

A reporter spoke to Reid on the phone. 'What time is the board going to convene for the test case?'

'Oh, the one the lawyers are talking about?' Reid asked, innocence itself.

'Yes.'

'Well, there is some talk of one at 11 o'clock.'

At noon he was asked the same question.

'We may go on with it right away.'[15]

He had fought for thirty-five days to avoid this. Now the machinery of justice was thrown into motion.

6

THE COURT OF APPEAL

Bird decided that Munshi Singh was the best candidate and brought him before the Board of Inquiry at 12.30. Malcolm Reid with inspectors Howard and Elliott comprised the panel. Hopkinson and the assistant interpreter, Harry Gwyther, stood by to give evidence.

Munshi Singh, from the village of Gulpur in the Hoshiarpur district of the Panjab, was a 26-year-old married man whose wife and daughter were left in India. Like many of his fellow passengers, he knew only a little English and he gave his answers in Panjabi. He said that he had tried to come directly from Calcutta to Vancouver, but had been refused a ticket by steamship companies in Calcutta and had come on to Hong Kong. There he had learned of the *Komagata Maru*, already on her way, and had caught up with her in Yokohama. He said he was a farmer and he told the Board that, with his brother, he owned seven pieces of land, the largest the size of a large double lot in Vancouver. As soon as he found a suitable tract of land he intended to wire home for the money so he could farm in British Columbia. Bird asked him why he had come to Canada and the interpreter gave his reply: 'To do work on farms to purchase some land and do work on farms.' Harry Gwyther broke in: 'He did not say that— ask him again.' And Munshi Singh answered for himself in English. 'To do farming.'[1]

Munshi Singh had left Yokohama with £9 after spending £20 on his ticket. He now had £6, equivalent to $30, and he showed the Board six gold sovereigns. Bird asked him the value of his property in India. Twenty-five thousand rupees, over $8,000. Why didn't he bring more money with him? Through the interpreter came the reply: 'He says "I am not educated: I may not transfer my money to banks; and I have not brought much money

The passengers dressed to go ashore, 23 May 1914—Gurdit Singh, foreground left, with his son, Balwant, and, to his left, Daljit Singh. Vancouver Public Library, No. 6231 (VPL 6228)

H.H. Stevens, centre, meets the press on board the tug *Sea Lion*, with Malcolm Reid standing third from left, and Hopkinson on extreme right. Vancouver Public Library, No. 6228 (VPL 6228)

Scene in Vancouver Harbour, 21 July 1914. HMCS *Rainbow* called to aid in deporting passengers on board *Komagata Maru*. Photo by W.J. Moore. City Archives, Vancouver

so that I may not be looted in the way as I have to pass from the different countries." '

It was a good answer. Many of Munshi Singh's compatriots, in similar circumstances, made poor witnesses because they did not understand the purpose of the questions put to them and would insist on stories palpably false or suppress evidence in their favour. He, himself, was as close to unprepared as a witness could be. Brought ashore that morning, interviewed through an interpreter by a lawyer he had never seen before, and then rushed straight into this hearing, his understanding of what was going on was imperfect at best. As he entered the room where the inquiry was being held, Husain Rahim and some other local Indians tried to approach him but were kept away. The only man there that he knew at all well was his interpreter, Bhan Singh, a fellow passenger, the school teacher and friend of Rughunath Singh. Hopkinson and Gwyther listened closely to what passed between them and were quick to accuse Bhan Singh of coaching when he was too elaborate in explaining a question.

When it came to cross-examination, the Department's lawyer, H. W. D Ladner, one of Robie Reid's junior partners, put on Munshi Singh the burden of proof.

'Have you got any evidence at all that you can give to substantiate your statements that the Company in Calcutta refused to give you a ticket to Vancouver?'

'He has . . .'

'What?'

'As there was no one with him he cannot produce any witness.'

'The same thing I suppose applies to the statement he made about when he left India—he cannot corroborate that in any way?'

'There are villagers in India can tell.'

'They are not here?'

'No.'

'He cannot corroborate the statement as to his money possessions—the statement made here today about his money possessions cannot be corroborated?'

'He has evidence in his village.'

'He has none here?'

'No.'

That was the heart of the examination and with that Ladner

5

rested his case. A motion to reject Munshi Singh's application and
to hold him for deportation was quickly passed, and Bird went
straight off to a Supreme Court judge to obtain a *pro forma*
refusal of a writ of habeas corpus. That night, accompanied by
Ladner, he took the ferry for Victoria, preparing himself for the
Court of Appeal.

The people on the *Komagata Maru,* including Gurdit Singh,
were confused by what had taken place, unaware that their friends
on shore had agreed to a test case, and, therefore, suspicious of
the whole proceeding.² Everything that Bird did was done on
behalf of the passengers, but not necessarily with their consent.
He took his instructions from Rahim, and while letters went back
and forth, the officials who carried them intercepted and read
what they pleased. Without any other kind of communication,
the passengers were pretty much in the dark.

That evening they sent a wire to the Governor–General:
'Many requests to Immigration Department for water but useless
better order shoot than this miserable death.' Rahim and Bhag
Singh had tried to make arrangements with Gardner Johnson but
could not provide immediate payment and nothing went out that
night. On the morning of the 26th, Reid still saw no reason to
do anything, and, later on, when the Japanese brought aboard a
barrel of water for themselves, some of the passengers fell on it,
snatching at it, spilling it, licking water from the deck. Bhan
Singh and Pohlo Ram, perhaps pressurized by the others, penned
a note to Reid saying that if water was not supplied within an
hour, 'a few passengers would breathe their last'. No water came.
Not until the 27th did Gardner Johnson accept Rahim's promise
of payment and produce 103 tonnes.³

The local Indians had sent messages to the Maharajas of Patiala
and Nabha, Sikh states in the Panjab, and to the Khalsa Diwan
and the Singh Sabha throughout the Panjab. Meetings had been
held at Lahore, Amritsar, and Delhi, and others were planned to
protest against the Canadian and Indian government policies in
this affair. As a speaker at the Lahore meeting said, Canada must
be made to understand that she is not dealing with a few hundred
men only, but with 330 million Indians. Why were the Japanese
and Chinese allowed to enter the Dominion while Indian subjects of His Majesty's Empire were not? The men on the *Komagata Maru* were now on the verge of starvation. Why had the

Government of India taken no steps to relieve the situation?[4]

Although the Anglo-Indian press took the Canadian side, the Government of India watched with apprehension and the Viceroy expected trouble in the Panjab if stories of police brutality came back from Canada.[5] His concern was relayed to the Canadian government by the British Colonial Secretary and to Reid by Superintendent Scott: 'Home authorities anxious that force shall not be used unless absolutely necessary to prevent illegal entry of Hindus.' Reid was sure that he and his officers had acted with the utmost tolerance, and, although he promised to use every ounce of discretion and diplomacy, he repeated his warning about riots if the passengers were landed, and disclaimed all responsibility if that should happen.

The case of Munshi Singh was argued in the Court of Appeal at Victoria on Monday and Tuesday, 29 and 30 June.[6] J. Edward Bird and Robert Cassidy, a well-regarded local lawyer, a man of 60, long resident in Vancouver, appeared for Munshi Singh. W. B. A. Ritchie and W. H. D. Ladner represented the immigration agent. Both sides had to prepare in a hurry; and on the Indian side it showed. 'I came into this case at a very late date . . .', said Cassidy, more concerned about his own reputation than the fate of his clients, 'I had not time to read.' The local Indians had tried to get T. R. E. MacInnes, a lawyer long interested in the Indian question, and, failing him, the firm of McCrossan and Harper, advocates in a number of Indian cases including Rahim's. Both refused, McCrossan and Harper explaining that, in their view, the whole affair had got 'beyond the realm of legal proceedings' and had become a question of national policy and diplomacy rather than law.

Cassidy, the third choice, brought in at the last minute, argued more or less off the cuff, leaving the Immigration Act alone, concentrating on the three orders-in-council, P.C. 23, P.C. 24, and P.C. 897.

Section 37 of the Act stated:

> Regulations made by the Governor in Council under this Act may provide as a condition to permission to land in Canada that immigrants and tourists shall possess in their own right money to a prescribed minimum amount, which amount may vary according to the race, occupation or destination . . .

P.C. 24 imposed a $200 minimum for Asian immigrants but no

minimum for tourists or non-Asian immigrants, and Cassidy tried
to make something of that, insisting that some amount would
have to be specified for every class of immigrant and tourist. It
was a fragile point.

Turning to P.C. 23, the continuous passage order, he pounced
on the term *all immigrants*—a general prohibition, he said, and
quite a different thing to 'any immigrant', the words used in the
Act. He tried to tell the judges that the Act could be applied only
in individual cases, and that an order prohibiting the landing of
all immigrants who came otherwise than by continuous passage
was improper. But he offered nothing to support his view beyond
a close reading of the section of the Act in question. The terms
any immigrant and *any person* appeared throughout the Act, but
Cassidy did not attempt to show that they were used consistently
in the sense of his interpretation.

When he came to P.C. 897, the order prohibiting the landing
of labourers at British Columbian ports, he wanted to argue that
Munshi Singh had sworn he was a farmer and intended to farm
and that the immigration authorities had no evidence to the
contrary. It was not a simple matter to make this case out because
it involved a review of the evidence taken by the Board of
Inquiry, and Section 23 of the Immigration Act stated that no
court had jurisdiction to 'review, quash, reverse, restrain or otherwise interfere with any proceeding, decision or order' of a Board
of Inquiry given within the authority of the Act. One could ask
if the Board had gone outside its authority or if the Act or the
orders-in-council were good; but that was all.

Cassidy, trying to bring the matter in by the back door, said
that no act could empower the Board to make a false finding of
fact, and that, if the Board were going to deport a man as a
labourer, they had to have a reason for believing that he was a
labourer. Otherwise, said Cassidy, the Board had no jurisdiction,
and their decision was subject to review by the Court. Munshi
Singh was being deported simply because the Board said they did
not believe him. 'Why, they could deport anybody. All that had
to be done is for them to catch you, and you tell all about yourself and you swear that you are not a labourer and they immediately find that you are, and deport you.' The judges were not
impressed by this argument, although they listened to it for over
an hour. The onus was on Munshi Singh to show that he was not

a labourer, said Mr Justice Galliher. He had not produced any documents or witnesses to support his story. The Board had not been satisfied. 'Can we say they acted without jurisdiction?'

Bird took over in the afternoon, tackling the Immigration Act itself. His principal contention was that Canada did not have the right to exclude British subjects because the British–North America Act did not give her that power. Canada could legislate on the subject of aliens; that had been established. But there had been no case yet tried or decided which dealt with a British subject's right of entry.

Could we not keep out murderers?—he was asked. Yes, he conceded, Canada could do that; it could pick its immigrants. Mr Justice Martin referred to Section 3 of the Act which prohibited the insane, diseased, crippled, criminal, and vagrant. Canada could refuse entry to these people even if they were British subjects, he observed. If one class of British subjects could be stopped, why not another? By now Bird was floundering. Earlier in the summer, he had sounded extremely confident of his chances in court, if he could get to court. Now he abandoned the heart of his case in confusion, indicating that he was ready to move on to his next point. The judges assured him that they wanted him to have every opportunity to make his case. He protested: 'This matter has been rushed along'; asked for permission to consult senior counsel —an empty request since Cassidy had already disclaimed any knowledge of the subject—and went on to assert that it should be held illegal to 'impose in Canada a penalty for belonging to a British race', an absurd statement because nowhere in the Act were British subjects singled out. He was extemporizing badly and the judges questioned him no further.

The next day, hot and heavy in the courtroom, Bird plunged on, openly groping for arguments. 'I have sought them in all directions', he said at one point. He caused the greatest stir when he brought forth an encyclopedia to prove that *Asiatic race* was a misnomer and that an order-in-council referring to an 'Asiatic race' was defective. He tried to show that the Immigration Act impinged on Magna Charta because it provided for detention and deportation without judgment by peers. He argued that Munshi Singh, a British subject, coming directly from Hong Kong, a British territory, had met the requirement that he came by continuous passage from his native country. He observed that civil rights lay within provincial jurisdiction and he claimed that deportation deprived Munshi Singh of his civil rights and that the Federal Act authorizing deportation was *ultra vires*. At every stage he met a barrage of questions from the bench, questions that cut away at his arguments. Twice he had to be reminded to stay away from ground already covered by Cassidy. Finally, as if driven to make the worst of his case, he ended his presentation disputing Mr Justice MacDonald's unimpeachable principle that it was the prerogative of the court 'to declare the law, not to make it'.

For the government, Ritchie, tall, thin, and elderly, went through the bulk of his argument without interruption, his points supported far more extensively in precedents in the law. By the time he was finished, 71 volumes from the law library lay spread across the tables. Either he was better prepared or he had an easier case. He went straight to the defence of the Immigration Act. Section 95 of the British–North America Act gave Canada the power to regulate immigration; immigration meant immigration from all parts of the world; if it had not been intended to give Canada control over British immigration, then the term alien immigration would have been used; that was the expression employed in imperial statutes. If there was any question of Canada's power to restrict the rights of British subjects by reason of their race, one had only to take the example of the native Indian; it had been done with them. If the Act infringed on provincial legislation in the area of civil rights, that did not make it unconstitutional as long as it lay within a clearly spelled-out field of federal jurisdiction. Magna Charta was not affected. The Immigration Act was the law of the land and the immigration officers had acted within that law. Munshi Singh could not claim that he was being held outside the law.

When he came to the arguments against the orders-in-council, the judges began to interrupt, but it was not hard to see that they were accepting his points and simply hurrying him over the self-evident ground and probing him on what was more complex. He took some time to answer Cassidy's claim that the Board of Inquiry had made a false finding when it declared Munshi Singh a labourer; and he spent even longer replying to Cassidy's elaborate attack on the language of the order imposing a $200 requirement; but he passed quickly over the arguments against the continuous passage order; gave short shrift to the definition of the term Asiatic race—'my friend cannot search books of ethnology as to the derivation of words, because the law we are governed by is that statutes are governed by the popular construction of words'; and dismissed in a couple of sentences the idea that a British subject born in India could be considered a native of all parts of the British Empire. There were a great many other points, he said, that had been 'mooted with more or less degree of confidence' by the junior counsel for Munshi Singh; but he would not deal with them. 'I think they carry their answer with their presentation.'

Judgment was reserved till the following Monday, but Bird must have come away knowing he had lost. In the interval, a stubborn situation had developed on the ship. The passengers had exhausted the provisions sent out on 11 June by the Shore Committee. As long as they had cash in their pockets, they could ask the immigration officers to go into town to purchase food for them; and, on an individual basis, Vancouver Sikhs were bringing food to the Immigration Office.[7] No one was starving, but the passengers were living from meal to meal and a number went to Gurdit Singh for the money they had given him in Moji. He said they would get it when they landed.

That was the state of affairs when four Indians, three from the town of Nanaimo, came to the Immigration Office on Friday morning, 3 July, wanting to see friends on the ship who had complained that Gurdit Singh was keeping their money. This was the kind of grousing that the immigration officials liked to encourage, and they took the visitors out to the *Komagata Maru* in a launch. As they pulled alongside, a host of passengers came to the rail shouting and singing. Conversation was impossible, and as the friends of the people from Nanaimo stepped out on the gangway, Gwyther, the Assistant Hindi Interpreter, decided to let them onto the launch. There were five of them. Gurdit Singh, watching, was aware that one of the Sikhs employed by the Immigration Department was related to one or two of the passengers who had been allowed onto the launch, and he thought that the five had gone to sign some trumped-up document.[8] It smelled of conspiracy and he ordered the gangway raised, leaving the five on the launch.

They had to stay there overnight. On Saturday morning, Reid

and Hopkinson cornered Captain Yamamoto who had spent the
night on shore, enjoying a liberty denied all of the passengers
and most of the crew. They wanted Yamamoto to call in the
police, muster his crew, and put the five on by force. He was in
command, not Gurdit Singh. 'When the captain says the gangway is to be put down, anyone who interferes is obstructing the
commander', they told him.[9]

Yamamoto, through an interpreter, asked for time, a day, to
talk to Gurdit Singh. He said that the passengers were very
excited and that Gurdit Singh had no sense and sometimes looked
'like he was out of his mind a little bit', but that he would obey
a ruling of the Court and that the passengers were already packing
to go.

The officials were certain that the laws of Canada meant nothing
to the Sikhs and that they would try to jump ship if they lost
their case in court. Still rankling was the memory of last November's escape from the Victoria detention shed. That was why
Reid viewed the five stranded passengers so grimly. His authority
was being tested. He had enough sense to allow the captain forty-
eight hours, but he did not expect any results.

That morning, Yamamoto had gone to Rahim's office in China-
town to get a note for Gurdit Singh, a subversive act as far as
the officials were concerned. Hopkinson learned about it from
Yoshi, the department's Japanese interpreter. He had already
learned of the dinner given at Shimonoseki in April by Sato and
other Japanese businessmen and of the speeches they had made
associating themselves with Gurdit Singh's enterprise. These scraps
of evidence gave birth to a very sinister picture. That afternoon
Hopkinson sent Yoshi off to find out more, and Yoshi, entering
a Chinese restaurant, overheard Yamamoto and Japanese Consul,
Y. A. Hori, in an adjoining box. They were asking themselves:
should the captain admit that he could not control the passengers?
Would it be better to admit or not? 'If the time came', said Hori,
putting prudence ahead of pride, 'it would be better to admit.'
They noticed Yoshi, and when he came over to ask why the
captain had gone to Rahim, Yamamoto explained that he had
picked up a note to pacify the passengers. He would show it to
the immigration authorities before he went on board. All this
Yoshi reported to Hopkinson. It showed that Yamamoto had an
instinct for self-preservation. But Reid and Hopkinson imagined

that a deeper plot—an international Japanese–Indian conspiracy—lurked beneath the surface.[10]

The five displaced passengers—the 'lonely Singhs' the reporter for the evening paper called them—slept Friday, Saturday, and Sunday nights on the top deck of the immigration department's launch *Winamac*. During the day they were kept on the smaller launch and for a period they were deposited in the harbour on a large wooden buoy used for tying up coal hulks. On Monday morning, Reid was ready to call in the police and he spoke to Gardner Johnson in Yamamoto's presence. However, Johnson took the captain's side. He thought the passengers would back down once they knew the Court's decision. 'They think word may come to allow them to come ashore.'[11]

Late in the morning, the Court of Appeal brought in its verdict. All five judges upheld the Immigration Act and the orders-in-council. Munshi Singh's appeal was dismissed.

Reid went out in the *Winamac* in the afternoon, taking Bird with him. They found the passengers ready for trouble, carrying clubs fashioned from driftwood they had fished up from the sea, still unwilling to take the five men back. During the morning, when the immigration launch had approached the wharf, two or three hundred white men, seeing the five and thinking that the Indians had won in court and were being landed, had lined the shore, shouting and gesturing. All this added to Reid's excitement. It was Bird, addressing the passengers from the top of the *Winamac's* house deck, who broke the bad news. The court had gone against them. They had lost their case.

Reid went straight to the Mayor of Vancouver who promised as many police as were required. When Captain Yamamoto and Consul Hori refused to authorize the use of force, Reid delivered a letter to the Captain saying, in effect, that by failing to co-operate, he had made himself an accomplice in a breach of the Immigration Act. Then at a little after 8 in the evening, with a crowd collected along the waterfront to see the action, Reid returned to the *Komagata Maru*. The rope ladder was already hanging over the side, so it was obvious that the passengers did not intend to fight. Gurdit Singh wanted to talk. 'Now I'll give you two minutes more in which to make up your minds', Reid shouted from the launch. 'At the end of two minutes I'll send for the police.'[12]

Gurdit Singh threw up his hands and the five climbed aboard. As far as Reid was concerned, the threat had made all the difference.

In the beginning, Gurdit Singh had declared he would battle right through to the highest court of appeal, the Judicial Committee of the British Privy Council. But it was not realistic to carry on. The Supreme Court of Canada would not be sitting until October and there would be immense problems in trying to go directly to the Committee of the Privy Council in the current calendar year. The decision of the Court of Appeal meant defeat for the passengers and the Indian community in Canada.

7

FORCE

Piles of garbage and debris, the accumulation of several weeks, lay on the decks of the *Komagata Maru*. Hopkinson had had a look around on the 3rd and had reported that the ship was ripe for an epidemic, but nothing had been done to clean it up. It was a question of responsibility. Who should pay? No one remarked that these passengers who had participated in what Reid called 'a deliberate and flagrant attempt to evade our laws' were carefully observing a local regulation against jettisoning garbage.

Having lost in the Court of Appeal, would they go home without a fuss? Bird went out to see Gurdit Singh the next day, Tuesday, 7 July, for their second meeting and their first in private —a meeting permitted by Reid under pressure from his own counsel.[1] The lawyer came back with a letter signed by Gurdit Singh and a committee of five representing the passengers.

J. E. Bird,
  We hereby instruct you to waive Board of Enquiry for all on Board *Komagata Maru* and to negotiate for return of *Komagata Maru* to Hong Kong under either plans discussed or any arrangements you may make.

The doctor, Rughunath Singh, had not agreed, claiming non-immigrant status, but the majority of the passengers, viewing him as a traitor, were determined that he should go back with them. Bhan Singh and one other passenger who also had hopes of going ashore kept quiet for a moment, intimidated by the rest. Gurdit Singh himself wanted special permission to disembark in Vancouver with his six-year-old son so they could return by way of London, spending no more than two weeks in Canada on the way. No one else asked to be landed.

The question was how they were to go back and who was to put up the money. Bird argued that the government should deal with the co-charterers, Rahim and Bhag Singh, in the same way that it did with any shipping line. Just because these men had a personal interest as members of the Indian community, the government had no right to trample over their separate interest as businessmen. There was coal on board which they wanted to unload and lumber which they wished to take on. If the authorities allowed the *Komagata Maru* to dock, the charterers would bond the passengers against escape. Alternatively, they would waive their right to take on cargo and the ship could be ready to sail in twenty-four hours, or at least by the end of the week, if the government agreed to pay their fares to a total of $20,000.

Bird insisted that his clients had come in good faith and deserved consideration. They had been encouraged by the fact that their ship had been allowed to leave Hong Kong after the Governor had cabled Canada for information and by the opinion of a Hong Kong law firm whose letter stated that there were no restrictions on Indians who wished to travel to Vancouver 'so far as this Colony was concerned'. Gurdit Singh had waited until now to bring this letter out and Bird lost no time in giving it to the press. Of course it referred only to Hong Kong regulations governing emigration and said nothing about Canadian law, but it was an open question whether or not Gurdit Singh had misread it. The Sikh leader also produced a bank book showing more than $9,000 on deposit in Japan, evidence, he thought, that put the authorities in a bad light for refusing to let him come ashore to conduct business.

The evening paper suggested that Canadians could afford to be magnanimous. 'Mr Gurdit Singh has given up the fight and is going home. It will probably be agreed that he is a good sports-man and has played his game to the limit. ... When a man is defeated and meets his defeat without making a fuss it is only sportsmanlike to realize his conquerors bear him no ill will. ... Canada bears Mr Gurdit Singh no grudge for having done his best.'[2]

But Reid did not trust Gurdit Singh, or Bird, or especially Husain Rahim. 'My reply to Mr Bird', he wrote to the Superintendent of Immigration, 'is to strengthen our guard. ...' He saw the request to dock as a ruse and the offer to waive Boards of Inquiry as a cover for plans to escape ashore. As far as he was concerned, Gurdit Singh had been aware of the law and had intended to get around it. And knowing that the charterer had

$9,000 tucked away in Japan, Reid objected to spending government money 'unless absolutely necessary'. Sections 44 and 45 of the Immigration Act thrust the responsibility for feeding and transporting deported immigrants on the shipping companies that brought them, and Reid thought that these sections should be enforced if it was at all possible.

There was some nasty work going on Reid was sure. Gurdit Singh's friends on shore were known seditionists. Rahim had arrived in Canada carrying instructions for bomb manufacture in his pocket. And at that very moment the immigration agent thought he had evidence that these people were plotting his own murder.

On Wednesday, 8 July, two days after the decision in the Court of Appeal, one of Hopkinson's informants reported a conversation which he said he had overheard on the street at 3 p.m. that afternoon between Rahim, Sohan Lal, and Mohammed Akbar, three members of the Shore Committee.[3]

> Mohammed Akbar: What do you think about Mr Reid and Hopkinson?
> Sohan Lal: Both of these persons are great robbers. All our hopes and works we intend are ruined.
> Rahim: It is a shame for us, there are so many Hindus here. If two or three will die for them it will not be a bad thing to do.
> Mohammed Akbar: We ought to talk this matter over in the Committee, and I will get one man ready for this work; but that man is too greedy.
> Rahim: Then we can pay him two or three thousand dollars by collections. You get that man ready.
> Mohammed Akbar: Very well, I will try for this.
> Sohan Lal: I think I will try to get one man ready. We ought to tell about this in Committee.
> Rahim: Be careful, don't let anyone hear about it.
> Mohammed Akbar: I think we ought to speak to Bhag Singh first privately, and then discuss in Committee.
> Rahim: What do you think about this, Sohan Lal?
> Sohan Lal: As you say.
> Rahim: We will see Monday, and also arrange for prize on Monday.
> Sohan Lal: Don't you think Mohammed Akbar Shah will do this work.
> Rahim: No, he can't but we will get some rogue whitemen from Socialist Party. I will see and let you know if I can get some.
> Mohammed Akbar: Well, I am going. See you Monday.
> *Bande Mataram.*

Reid had also learned that Indians in Victoria were trying to make bombs, that there had been an attempt to buy twenty-five automatic pistols at a Victoria hardware store, and that there was a plan to buy pistols in Port Angeles in the State of Washington. He had known for some time that certain Indians were looking for weapons and talking darkly of what they intended to do. Three weeks earlier, one of Hopkinson's men, Bela Singh, had been offered real estate, or a ticket to India and $500 by a local Sikh, Mewa Singh. He was to stay away from the Immigration Office. 'Otherwise', said Mewa Singh, 'if you do not leave, the Hindus will shoot you and the whole Immigration Department....'⁴ Violent language did not necessarily lead to violent deeds, but Reid took it seriously. He was the object of great hatred and was afraid. No one could have convinced him that the men he dealt with were good sportsmen or deserved a scrap of consideration.

Throughout the summer, the Superintendent of Immigration, W. D. Scott, had allowed Reid to set his own course, and while day by day and even hour by hour telegrams and letters came in from Reid reporting on the situation, Scott knew far less than he should have. Nobody in Ottawa had taken the measure of Reid's tactics while he played for time during the first four weeks the ship was in harbour. One might say that Scott preferred not to know too much, except that his tone, when he learned the truth, was much sharper than it might have been. Reid now wanted to deport the passengers without Boards of Inquiry because he was afraid of further delay. But the Act said that to deport you had to hold a Board of Inquiry. 'I am unable to agree with Mr Reid's suggestion', Scott advised the Minister of the Interior. 'In the face of repeated instructions to complete Boards of Inquiry, I am at a loss to understand why it has not already been done.'⁵

The answer was simple. Reid had not wanted to give his opponents a chance in court. Now he had to get on with the job as quickly as he could, and, instead of shuttling the passengers in groups from ship to shore, he took his Board out to them. On Thursday afternoon, 9 July, he climbed the gangway with Inspectors Hopkinson, Howard, and Elliott; the Department's lawyer, W. H. D. Ladner; a lawyer for the immigrants, Mr Pratt of Bird's office; and two lady stenographers. He should have brought provisions as well. The water pumped on board on 27 June had run out on Tuesday and the passengers claimed that they had been without food since Monday morning. For three days they had been asking for help, but, up to the hour that Reid and his party pushed their way through an agitated throng from the gangway to the saloon, nothing had been done in response.

Gurdit Singh and his secretary, Daljit Singh, summoned to the saloon and told that the government was going to conduct Board of Inquiry hearings, refused to co-operate, unwilling to see the two tell-tales, Rughunath Singh and Bhan Singh landed when the rest were being turned back. Hopkinson tried to justify the procedure to the whole body of passengers gathered on the afterdeck, but there was no break in their ranks and when he called for a show of hands, no one would go before the Board. Rughunath Singh had been locked in his cabin so he had no vote. However, now that Reid was on the ship, where he had not been seen for a long time, some spokesmen suggested he should hear them out and he agreed to meet their committee in the saloon. At Hopkinson's suggestion, the stenographers took notes. At the onset, Reid was warned by the passengers that they were ready to launch the lifeboats and head for shore if provisions were not brought out by 9 p.m. He could search the ship for himself right then and there to see whether they had anything to eat or drink.

Reid did not want to pursue the matter. 'It is not necessary to search the ship. I have already interviewed the Mayor on their behalf. We will try and adjust the matter as soon as possible. If possible, tonight.'[6]

Hopkinson interpreted. 'They want to know what the Mayor said.'

'He said he would have to consult the Japanese Consul.'

This was not the way to placate anyone. One of the Committee spoke directly to Reid in English. 'For three days this matter had been going on, and we are starving. If a continuation of consultations go on we are likely to be starving by the time action is taken.'

Reid said that if the problem was not solved that night, it would be the next morning. Their lawyer, Bird, was working on it. The authorities would do the best they could to get water right away, but it was late. 'How much water do they want until tomorrow? We can get that at once.'

Amar Singh Nihang of the Lahore District turned on Reid.

'I would like you to be in the same position as we have been here for the past three days without water and see how you feel about it individually, and what must be the case of men collectively as in this case. You are getting your food three times a day, and your water. We are getting nothing. If you were starving for three or four hours you would soon take action to get something for yourself, but we have had nothing for three days or so.

'You have come to this boat possibly three times from the time she has been here. We have addressed you letters and complaints with regard to several matters. We have made enquiries for you from your officers that have come on this boat, but they have always said, "Mr Reid is attending to the matter," or "I do not know." You have never put in an appearance on this boat except on the three occasions and now as you are here we would like to hold you until such time as your promise of the sending of provisions and water is fulfilled.'

It says much for the demeanour of the passengers during the preceding seven weeks that Reid had dared come aboard with women in his party. Even now, when the stenographers were sent back to the safety of the launch, there was no attempt to stop them. Yet members of the press, later trying to find out what had happened, were told that the passengers had been close to violence and that one or two dangerous moments had been defused only by Hopkinson's diplomacy. Reid took the Sikh's words for a threat. He believed that his way out of the saloon by the principal exit was being blocked, and, with as much dignity as he could muster, he stepped out of the back door and shouldered through the mob on the deck to the gangway. He was back in the launch three hours after he had left it, having taken Hopkinson's advice to offer a temporary supply of food and water.[7]

True to his word, Reid returned in the evening with several of his officers, an inspector from the city police, and a cargo of flour, cabbages, and water, enough for a day and a half. From the launch he explained that the government had not backed down and that responsibility for provisioning still lay with the owners, the charterers, and the captain. He said he was sorry that the passengers had been misled by lawyers in Hong Kong and Vancouver with promises that they would win in the courts, and he warned them that they were subject to the laws of the city and the authority of the local police. Then he ordered the provisions put on board. Newsmen who had come out in a rowboat were struck by the passengers' good temper once they had food. A reporter for the *News-Advertiser* managed to get onto the steamer, the first newspaperman to have done so since its arrival. He walked from stem to stern, looking down one of the hatches at the rows of bunks far below, glancing into the temple where several people were praying, and finding the ship much cleaner and the smell of the garbage piled on the deck and covered with ashes much less obnoxious than he had been led to expect. The passengers were not exactly affable nor were they forbidding. He asked Daljit Singh—a slight, intense, young man—which person he felt most unfriendly towards. The answer was conciliatory, although it disguised much. 'We have no cause to complain of the attitude and treatment accorded us by the Canadian people. We feel we have been given a just hearing before the courts and we have no complaint. But we are most unfriendly towards our own government in not being strong enough to see that the Hindus as British subjects are allowed to go any place within the Empire.'[8]

The callousness of the civic and federal officials disturbed at least one editorialist.[9] Reid had shown himself indifferent to the welfare of the passengers and for no good reason because the government gave nothing away by ordering supplies. It could still take action against the owners to recover the cost. In fact Reid delivered the bill to Captain Yamamoto the next morning. In a letter to the Deputy Minister explaining what had been done, Hopkinson said that he was sure the government did not want the passengers to starve. It was remarkable that he should have had any doubt. He was worried about the possibility of a further more serious confrontation encouraged and exploited by Indian radicals both on shore and on the boat. 'I am using my best endeavours to avoid any physical clash between the passengers and the Government officials', he wrote, obliquely criticizing Reid.[10]

On Friday, 10 July, the fourth day following the court decision, deportation papers were prepared citing the passengers' refusal to appear for examination. As yet no arrangements had been made to provision the ship for her return, although people close to the situation could see that the government was going to have to do it. Unfortunately, the officials in Ottawa were not so perceptive, and Reid was not the man to straighten them out. He was absorbed by the manoeuvres of Rahim and Bhag Singh, who were seeking more than enough to recoup the money they had spent and threatening court action to arrest the ship if their terms were not met. Some passengers had called out to small craft offering five pounds per man to take them ashore, and from the ship came stories of a plan to set the coal on fire to cover a mass escape. Reid expected no less and appeared to believe that the only answer was a show of strength.[11] For the men on the ship there were no assurances. They did not know whether they would be eating after twenty-four hours, let alone for the whole of the Pacific crossing.

Captain Yamamoto, presented with the bill for the small amount of food and water delivered on the 9th, went around to Sir Charles Hibbert Tupper, the counsel engaged for the owners by the agent Gardner Johnson. Tupper decided that the time had come to by-pass all the lesser players and to appeal directly to the Prime Minister, Sir Robert Borden. He was an old friend of Borden, a former law-partner and, more than that, he and his father had drawn Borden into politics and had pushed him into the leadership of the Conservative party. So he presumed nothing when he telegraphed Borden on Friday, 10 July, explaining that although his firm acted for the owners, 'I address you in my personal capacity.' There was an exchange of telegrams over the weekend, and by Tuesday Reid had been told to do what Tupper suggested. That meant delivering provisions to the *Komagata Maru* at a point beyond Canada's five-kilometre limit, 250 kilometres by sea from Vancouver. The idea was that the passengers should show good faith by going that far on a promise.

Since the 9th, Reid had ordered a few tonnes of water each day, although he had not paid any of the bills. On Saturday his officers had taken out another temporary supply of food, more flour, cabbages, and rice, ignoring most of a long list of items that the passengers had specifically requested. They complained most about having to do without butter—they needed it to cook—and about the kind of flour they were given, insisting that it was no good and made them sick. It was bread flour instead of the whole-wheat flour they needed to make chapattis. Nor were they getting enough water to drink and to cook their meals as well as to run the generator, and they had gone for three nights without lights.[12]

They reminded Reid of the health hazards on board, the increasing number of flies and rats around the refuse on the deck and the sickness already prevalent as a consequence of insufficient food and exercise. At length a Health Department official visited the ship. He reported:

I found a large accumulation of ashes and garbage on the upper deck. The toilets were exceedingly filthy and required flushing, but owing to the above accumulation flushing the latrines would only carry the filth into the ash pile.

Below deck the accommodation is crowded; the floors are filthy, and the Hindus, some of them being sick are expectorating over the floors.

I am of the opinion that it should be thoroughly cleansed and lime washed. Further, that if at all practicable the Hindus should be landed at a quarantine station and the vessel thoroughly fumigated, the woodwork scrubbed off and the bunks lime washed.

By Friday, 17 July, clearance and deportation papers had been prepared, and 425 tonnes of water pumped on board. Reid had not allowed the ship to dock and he had not negotiated terms with Rahim and Bhag Singh. He did not intend to do so. Nor had he yet purchased food. He was waiting until the last moment, and all that the passengers had to eat was the remnants of the $50 worth that had been supplied the previous morning. As it was, Reid regretted having to put the water on, but it would have been impossible to tow water scows out to the five-kilometre limit. 'Expect departure late this afternoon unless anything unforeseen happens to prevent', he wired Ottawa.

One last duty was to get Dr Rughunath Singh, his wife, and son from the ship. For them at least the ordeal was over. The doctor had been unpopular with his fellow passengers ever since he had talked to immigration officials. Gurdit Singh had warned Reid that if he wanted peace on the *Komagata Maru*, he should not give the doctor special treatment. And Rughunath Singh had complained repeatedly that his life was in danger, yelling to Reid through the window of his cabin where he had been locked during the Immigration Agent's visit on the afternoon of the 9th, and writing on the 11th: 'they may strike at any moment. . . . Have you no pity? For God's sake save me from this and send me from this ship.' Reid, taking this none too seriously, had provided the doctor with a whistle and instructions to blow it through his porthole if he was attacked so that the guards on the Immigration launches could come to the rescue. Now, six days later, he was safely on shore.[13] Bhan Singh and one other who had claimed non-immigrant status had been left behind.

All the necessary papers from customs and immigration were

taken to the *Komagata Maru* by the shipping agent, Gardner Johnson, along with instructions to weigh anchor and leave. Johnson spoke to the passengers, telling them he was sorry they were being sent back and explaining that there would be provisions for them once they reached the five-kilometre limit. They were sceptical and answered that they wanted supplies to last all the way to Calcutta, and that they did not trust the Canadian authorities. Around 7.30 in the evening Johnson returned to shore. His last word to the passengers was that they would be sent back by force if they did not take his advice and go on their own.

The ship did not move. The immigration officials and H. H. Stevens blamed Yamamoto, and the Prime Minister was so advised in a night lettergram from Stevens: 'I am convinced from the attitude of the Captain that he is in collusion with Gurdit Singh and is purposely deceiving the Government and the Immigration authorities.' After an unsuccessful appeal to the Japanese Consul, Mr Hori, to intervene, Reid went out to the *Komagata Maru* to speak to the Captain. The time was 1 a.m., but he found the passengers wide awake, patrolling the decks, and carrying clubs. They refused to lower the gangway, but, after some argument, produced the captain who had been asleep and who emerged on the deck half-dressed. 'If you can't do anything with the ship,' Reid told him, 'let me know.' Yamamoto answered that he could not do anything 'as there are many Hindus and I can't go today.' He went with Reid—the passengers warning him that he would not be allowed back on the ship that night—and at 3 a.m. was taken by taxi to Gardner Johnson's home south of Vancouver, where Reid and Stevens with the help of two government lawyers and Gardner Johnson tried to get him to call in the police. Yamamoto did not want the responsibility, and Reid at length decided that the time could be better used sleeping and adjourned the conversation until 9 a.m.

Reid and Hopkinson believed that the *Ghadr*ite leaders in Seattle and San Francisco had a hand in the whole affair and the suspicion was confirmed by news received that evening as they had waited futilely for the *Komagata Maru* to get up steam. A U.S. immigration officer had allowed four Sikhs to cross the border at Sumas, eighty kilometres from Vancouver, for a short visit to see a friend. A few hours later, one of the four was arrested coming through the woods by provincial police on the

British Columbia side. He was carrying two automatic revolvers and 300 rounds of ammunition apparently purchased in the United States. His friends were picked up by the American immigration authorities and automatic pistols and ammunition were found in their possession as well. The man they had met turned out to be Taraknath Das whose activities, both in Canada and the United States, had been watched by Hopkinson since 1908. Accompanying Taraknath had been none other than Bhagwan Singh Jakh, the priest thrown out of Canada in November 1913. After meeting the *Komagata Maru* in Yokohama, he had found his way to San Francisco by way of Honolulu.

The man arrested on the Canadian side was Mewa Singh, the messenger who, a few weeks earlier, had conveyed a threat to one of the Department's informants. Held on the American side were the priest, Balwant Singh, and his friend, Bhag Singh, the President of the Khalsa Diwan and the co-charterer of the *Komagata Maru*. With them was Harnam Singh of Victoria, another leading figure in the revolutionary party. There was no doubt in the minds of the officials that the weapons they had purchased had been destined for the *Komagata Maru*.[14]

Having had little sleep, Reid arrived at his office on Saturday morning well before his appointed interview with Captain Yamamoto. 'We are awaiting the arrival of the Captain of the ship,' he wrote for the record, 'when another discussion will take place, and some drastic final action will be taken to rid the harbour of this ship.' He had two means in mind to make the Captain co-operate: the threat of a heavy fine and the promise, if there was any more delay, that the government would rescind its offer of provisions. Yamamoto was given until 6 p.m. to decide what to do. Consul Hori, who was present for this meeting, objected, saying that he needed to consult the Japanese government, but Reid and his lawyers saw no need for that. 'Really', said Mr Ladner as the issue was pursued during a telephone conversation that afternoon, 'I do not see that the matter concerns your Government at all.'[15]

At 5.15 Yamamoto returned to the *Komagata Maru*. He had agreed to raise a red flag as a signal for the police if the passengers would not let him sail, but, as the launch pulled alongside, he thought better of it. 'If I go aboard the ship and put up the red flag, they are too many for me', he said to the officer beside him;

'You go back and ask Reid to get the police immediately, 200 if he can, but I cannot raise the red flag as I promised.'

Reid wanted to board the steamer while there was still some light, but on Saturday evening with a large force on duty in the city, the chief of police said that he had only ten men to spare. Boarding time was set at 1 a.m. Sunday morning when a large number of police would have finished their shift. Six thousand dollars worth of provisions, a thirty-day supply, were delivered to the pier to be loaded on the *Sea Lion,* the largest tug in the harbour. Among those hanging around the Immigration Office watching the activity was Dr Rughunath Singh. A reporter for the *Daily News-Advertiser* asked him whether the passengers were armed. They were not properly armed, but he believed they had a few revolvers and a large number of daggers.

Around 12.30 a body of 125 police arrived with the chief at their head impatient to get the job over with, because his men had been on duty all day or had just come on for the night and had been diverted from their normal rounds. Reid had already sworn in 35 special immigration officers and armed them with Ross rifles borrowed from the Seaforth Highlanders, his own militia regiment. The police carried revolvers and batons.

Just before 1 a.m. Hopkinson was allowed fifteen minutes for a last parley with the passengers. He drifted alongside the *Komagata Maru* in a small launch at 12.58, called out for Gurdit Singh, and was told by voices in the dark that the old man would not talk and that neither the ship nor the passengers would leave the harbour until they had permission in writing from Rahim and Bhag Singh or had spoken to them personally.

At 1 a.m. the police and the force that Reid had mustered boarded the tug *Sea Lion.* A number of newspapermen jumped on as well. H. H. Stevens went along as did W. H. D. Ladner, counsel for the Immigration Department. Hopkinson was signalled to return and at 1.15 the *Sea Lion* pulled away from the pier. Earlier in the evening Hopkinson had spoken out against any attempt to take the *Komagata Maru* at night. He was the only person there who saw the situation with the eyes of the Indian government and he was afraid that news of a clash would inflame opinion in the Panjab. It was part of Hopkinson's discipline to shun publicity and to submit to orders. He was never very free with his words to the press, and although in conversation with

his colleagues he would let slip his irritation with Reid, he kept
that out of his correspondence with Ottawa. That evening, in
complete opposition to Reid and Stevens, he satisfied himself by
handing them a signed statement setting out his views.[16] Reid
rather ineffectually suggested that the police should hold off until
there was more light, but McLennan, expecting no trouble, would
not wait. His men, assuming that a force of 160 would be more
than enough, embarked in high spirits as if this little outing had
been set up just as an entertainment.

A searchlight mounted on the *Sea Lion* illuminated a solid line
of passengers leaning over the rail, shouting and waving clubs.
One called out for Hopkinson in Panjabi and warned him that
his people were ready to fight. 'This ship is going to stay
here. She is not going to move. If you start a fight the Hindus
will show you how to fight. If you make fast we will jump into
your boat and fight you and take chances. The Hindus are not
afraid.' The tug was bound to the steamer by a grappling hook
in spite of the efforts of the passengers to knock it away. One
of them wielding an axe began to chop at the line. He would
have cut through it quickly enough, but the police had laid out
hose and started the pumps, and Chief McLennan holding the
nozzle directed a cold stream of water along the rail. The advantage was only momentary because the hose would not take the
full pressure of the pumps, and the passengers were prepared
with piles of coal, fire bricks, and scrap metal which they had
brought up from the hold. They stood five metres above the deck
of the *Sea Lion* and with that advantage loosed an unanswerable
storm on the people below. The special immigration officers,
standing in the bow of the tug were less exposed and escaped
serious injury, but the police were unprotected. One of them,
struck by a brick, fell unconscious. Four or five received scalp
wounds. Another was rendered helpless by a blow on the arm.
Glass flew as the windows of the tug were smashed, and several
people, including the tugboat captain, were cut about the face.
Chief McLennan stood his ground, manning the hose, but his
men instinctively tried to get out of range, and as they crowded
to the starboard side, the tug listed dangerously. There were
cries of 'Keep to the left or we shall sink.' Then there were angry
shouts: 'Get her away from the ship. Why the — doesn't the
captain move her?' A gunman identified by some as Harnam

Singh, one of the five members of the passengers' committee, fired four shots from the *Komagata Maru*, striking no one. The police had been ordered beforehand not to draw their revolvers and McLennan shouted at them to hold steady. About fifteen minutes after the bowline had been made fast, a police constable managed to sever it; the tug, looking as if it had run under a coal chute, pulled away while the passengers on the *Komagata Maru* cheered.

8

INTIMIDATION

Moments after returning to shore at 2 a.m., Stevens wired the Prime Minister: 'Hindus on ship apparently desperately revolutionary and determined to defy law. Absolutely necessary that strong stand be taken and would urge that *Rainbow* or some Naval Department vessel be detailed to take charge of situation.' The *Rainbow*, based at Esquimault, and the *Niobe* at Halifax, second-hand cruisers acquired from Britain in 1911, constituted the whole of Canada's navy in 1914. For several months the *Rainbow* had been riding at anchor, and, although she was scheduled shortly to sail for the Bering Sea to patrol international sealing waters, she was as yet unfit for duty and possessed a crew of only forty-seven men and officers. Seventy-six men were being transferred from the *Niobe* and by coincidence they were due to arrive in Vancouver on the afternoon of the 20th. The remainder of the crew were to be supplied by the British and had not yet been sent.[1] Undermanned and out of repair, the *Rainbow* was still the mightiest vessel available. She had been used in 1911 to intimidate strikers in Prince Rupert, and Stevens now wanted to use her against the Indians on the *Komagata Maru*.

Borden, exasperated by the delay in getting rid of the *Komagata Maru*, had privately decided that the Immigration Act would have to be amended so that more summary remedies could be adopted.[2] But he knew that the Colonial Secretary and the Indian Government were worried about the way his people were handling the incident. Bloodshed had to be avoided, and he did not feel he could rely on the judgement of the local immigration agent and the local M.P. After consulting his Solicitor-General, Arthur Meighen, in the absence of more senior cabinet colleagues, he decided to make the *Rainbow* available, but, at the same time, to wire his Minister of Agriculture, Martin Burrell, in his Okanagan

constituency. 'Think it highly desirable that you proceed immediately Vancouver and report on situation.'

On Sunday morning Borden could not find any naval officers in
Ottawa, but he managed to reach Douglas Hazen, Minister of
Marine and Fisheries, on board a steamer bound from Moncton
to Halifax. The Commander of the *Rainbow* was alerted in the
evening and word came back from him that the cruiser did not
handle easily and probably could not be used to board the *Komagata Maru*. 'But her presence might have moral effect', Hazen
reported. Borden, having learned that the available crew was very
small, got in touch with the Militia Department to arrange to
bring out militia from Vancouver as marines. On Monday morning divers inspected the cruiser's hull, finding it very dirty and
spotting a small leak, but pronouncing it in good shape. She
sailed for Vancouver that evening, making a slow crossing under
reduced pressure because her boilers had not been safety tested.

The passengers were hungry but defiant. 'If we tell you all our
troubles,' Daljit Singh wrote his friends in a note intercepted by
Immigration, 'it will be giving you trouble. They are trying to
deport us forcibly and they will tell you afterwards that the ship
was taken away by the passengers. About 1.30 this morning a
tugboat came full of Police and tried to get on board by intimidation and tried to capture Bhai Gurdit Singh. . . . With the help of
the Guru we won, and saved the honour of our flag. We are
ready to die and kill. We will not take the boat away without
your orders and then only when they put provisions and water
on the boat first.'[3] The passengers were busy all Sunday erecting
a barricade of timbers along the rails and replenishing their arsenal
of coal. With a ready barrage they kept at a distance the police
launches on watch that night. They warned the captain that if he
called in the police again, he would be responsible for loss of life
and limb. They had not been supplied with food since the 16th
when they had been given enough for one meal. 'We are all hungry since three days', they wanted the Shore Committee to know.
'Immigration want to take away the steamer, to kill us on the way
with hunger.'

Hopkinson, showing no fear, boarded the *Komagata Maru* on
Monday morning to deliver a telegram from the Governor-
General. He stayed briefly to talk while H. H. Stevens shouted
up instructions from the safety of the launch. The conversation

broke off with Hopkinson's promise that the passengers would get no food until they were in a more reasonable state of mind.

Reid sent two officers around to Rahim's office with a letter for him to sign authorizing the passengers to leave. They were to accept no argument, but to say: 'We wish you to sign this letter and then we are in a position to know where you stand. The Committee of the *Komagata Maru* claim that you are the last drawback to their departure and as they will not leave without your consent we now present this letter for your signature.' To no one's surprise, Rahim refused.

A militia force of 204 turned out at daybreak on Tuesday, 21 July, and, at 7 a.m., marched to a position just south of pier A at the western end of the C.P.R. dock system. By the time they had formed up, a large crowd had gathered along the waterfront. Shortly after 8.15 the cruiser came through the narrows and anchored a few hundred yards south-west of the *Komagata Maru*. Out went Reid, Stevens, and the militia officers to confer with the Commander of the *Rainbow*. He planned to run alongside the *Komagata Maru*, drop three gangplanks, and send his marines and the militia on board with fixed bayonets. There would be no firing unless the passengers were seen to have a considerable number of firearms. As far as anyone knew, they had only one revolver. If the passengers resisted he had two firehoses at each gangplank which he hoped would be eough to subdue them without injury. However, before launching an assault, it was agreed that there should be another attempt to get the co-operation of the local Indian Committee.

The *Rainbow* carried twelve heavy-calibre guns and a number of machine guns all of which had been hastily remounted or unplugged at the breech and muzzle the day before. The broadside guns pointing at the *Komagata Maru* were uncovered at about 10 a.m. 'It is just a big joke', said Husain Rahim, watching from the upper floor of the Metropolitan building where his lawyers had their offices. 'They could sink her with two shots.' He was just one of a host drawn to the windows of the principal city buildings overlooking the inlet. 'There is no use ringing up this office for business. All the clerks are in the windows.' The roofs of the post office and other large buildings near the water, and even some buildings further back, were congested with spectators. Thousands of people had gathered at the ends of the streets opening onto the harbour, and thousands more had pushed onto the wharves and piers. Vancouver had taken the day off to see the show.

Everyone who had a launch, a sailing-boat, or a canoe, had taken to the water, and each time the patrolling immigration launch and the tug *Sea Lion*, carrying thirty–five riflemen, was passed, there was some hazard. The occupants of small craft, told to keep out of range, nonetheless came close to the *Rainbow* and the *Komagata Maru* to chat with the sailors and to see what the Sikhs looked like. During the morning the passengers of the *Komagata Maru* were quiet; spirits were low; the men were fearful and some were running every hour to the latrines. At noon, while the children—there were four on board—played on the bridge, the rest held a meeting on the main deck at the stern. There were two village musicians on the ship, one with a *dhad*, a four-inch bongo drum, the other with a seven-string *sarangi*. They sang a patriotic song, a very fervent song, a war song, and raised the passengers' spirits. The song was an old, historical one which told of a hero who honoured the precept: 'If you have to give your head for a cause, don't hesitate.' A speaker got up to exhort them to fight as long as they could, and they all resolved that, when they could fight no longer, they would go down to the boiler room, pour oil on the coal and start a fire that would take their assailants with them.[4] Those who were watching from pleasure craft around the *Komagata Maru* could not understand the words being used, but had no doubt that this was a council of war and that the passengers were going to make a stand—or wanted everyone to think so.

Martin Burrell, the Minister of Agriculture, arrived from the Okanagan that morning and quickly briefed himself. He accepted Reid's view that something would have to be done to gain control of the ship before another day had passed. However, when he visited the *Rainbow*, Commander Walter Hose told him he would not be surprised if it cost a hundred lives to take the ship by force, and Burrell returned to shore late in the morning convinced that concessions would have to be made in the interest of peace.

He found himself in the midst of negotiations with the Indian Shore Committee who had been refusing to do anything to persuade their friends to go. At 11 a.m., Stevens and Reid sent Hopkinson off with a final ultimatum for the passengers, but he did not deliver it when a few local Indians offered to talk to Rahim. Around 11.30, Rahim was contacted by phone through A. H. MacNeill, the senior partner in the firm of MacNeill, Bird, Macdonald, and Darling which had been representing the Indians all summer. At the other end of the line, Burrell, Robie Reid, H. H. Stevens, and Malcolm Reid were in conference. Rahim now said he would take a delegation out to reason with the passengers if they were first given food. 'There is no use arguing with those hungry half-starved people until they have had food and have had time to consider.' Reid and Stevens were of a mind to make an end of it, and Burrell agreed; yet there was a great pile of provisions on the wharf and the Minister thought that some of these could be given to the passengers right away to ease the situation. Rahim and his Committee were told that they would be taken to the ship at once and would be allowed to take some of the Immigration Department's store of food with them, but they had to act by 1.30.

Shortly after the deadline, Rahim and nine of his Committee turned up at the Immigration building. They were shown the provisions. To intimidate them, Reid led them past the rows of militia standing with fixed bayonets along the wharf. The officials gave them an hour, Reid recording the time they boarded the *Komagata Maru* as 2.25. At the end of the hour they announced they had worked out a solution with Gurdit Singh but needed to go uptown to consult their solicitor. Some time before 5 p.m. they returned with MacNeill and a set of demands that, in spite of the six-inch guns on the *Rainbow* and the militia's naked bayonets, were no weaker than anything they had asked before. They had a list of provisions twice as long as the list Reid had already purchased. They said that the passengers wanted to be sent back to Calcutta, not Hong Kong. And they still expected the government to refund the money they had spent to meet the charter obligations.

All summer Reid had refused to make concessions, convinced that the passengers and Rahim and his friends would exploit every opening given. He lived in fear of his life; his family had been sent out of town; his house was guarded at night.[5] It was not surprising that Reid and his friend Stevens relied on intimidation rather than negotiation. However, Martin Burrell came onto the scene with a somewhat more open mind and real qualms about the use of force. He knew that the Prime Minister wanted the *Komagata Maru* to go with the least possible delay and no unnecessary violence, and he saw no virtue in quibbling over a few thousand dollars worth of provisions if that was an obstacle to settlement.[6] When the Committee pressed the point, Burrell gave way completely and approved their full list of provisions. He would not agree to sending the passengers back to Calcutta, but on the critical issue, that of the charter money, he tried to find a way to soften the government's position without actually promising to pay a penny. The answer was to offer to consider the Committee's claim, and he put this into writing for MacNeill to show his clients. The key sentence read: 'As a Member of the Government, I shall wire to the Prime Minister, asking that these claims should be thoroughly looked into by an imperial Commissioner and will urge that full and sympathetic consideration be given to all those who deserve generous treatment.' In return the passengers would have to agree immediately to give control of the ship to the captain and to return peacefully to Asia. Burrell had taken very little time to decide on these terms, and it was only a little after 5 p.m. when MacNeill closeted himself with the Committee to persuade them to give in.

It had been a slow afternoon for Vancouverites watching from the waterfront, but, afraid of missing something, they had not gone home; and nearby cafes were receiving a stream of small boys sent for food by older folk who were holding on to their vantage places. The harbour was as congested as ever, and the Australian liner, *Niagara*, arriving around 4 p.m., had difficulty making its way through the small craft to its berth. 'Immense crowds constantly on the waterfront and undoubtedly public sentiment will require an immediate solution', Martin Burrell had reported to the Prime Minister earlier in the day, reflecting the outlook of local officials who saw the danger of riots on shore as compelling reason for prompt action against the *Komagata Maru*. Journalists moving through the crowds found them impatient for a spectacle that had not yet come off—but people had come to watch, not to participate. Those on the water near the *Komagata Maru* provoked only grins and some banter among the Sikhs; and on shore there had been no commotion when a Sikh got up to speak in Panjabi before hundreds of people standing near the entrance to the C.P.R. depot.

At 5.30, it appeared that there would be action at last as the immigration launch *Winamac* headed out to the *Komagata Maru*. But the onlookers were to be disappointed. The Shore Committee had decided to accept Burrell's offer and were going out to tell the passengers. They had been on board for half-an-hour when Yamamoto appeared on the deck with the draft of a letter signed by Rahim, authorizing the captain to get up steam in preparation for departure. He ran down the steps of the gangway to show it to Stevens, Reid, Hopkinson, and the Militia Brigadier, J. Duff Stuart. Looking up, everyone could see whiffs of smoke from the smoke stack.

While the immigration launch was tied alongside the *Komagata Maru*, a number of the passengers asked good-naturedly who had been hurt and how seriously, during the encounter on Sunday morning, and expressed relief when immigration officials, whom they knew by name, indicated that they had suffered only minor injuries. Now that their terms had been met, they showed no hostility. As the launch drew away, they called out their farewells, and, apparently happy with the way the affair had been resolved, began to applaud enthusiastically.

Martin Burrell turned to Robie Reid, the government's legal counsel, and said, 'Mr. Reid, this is the most awful day in my life. Another day like this would kill me.' Reid replied, 'Mr Burrell, now you know something of what *we* have gone through for two long months.' And Burrell said, 'Mr Reid, *now* I know.'[7] In the eyes of the local officials, Burrell was an intruder, and, although an impasse had been broken within hours of his arrival, they would not admit to themselves or anyone else that his concessions had been instrumental. Burrell wired the Prime Minister to tell him the good news. 'Situation has been most anxious and critical,' he reported, 'but hope it is peace with honour.' Stevens sent a separate telegram attributing the result to the presence of the *Rainbow*. 'Quite convinced . . . that this fortunate ending could not have been reached unless display of force had been used such as we requisitioned this brought leaders to their senses and once they gave in others were like children.'

At the same time, the Shore Committee were wiring their *Ghadr* friends in San Francisco: 'Fearless passengers repulsed first midnight attack, and were ready to face Marines today but settlement effected by Hindoo Committee to avoid bloodshed. Immi-

gration will provision ship tomorrow for return voyage. People
laughed bringing Cruiser against unarmed passengers. This in-
humane treatment to be known all over. Ship may sail tomorrow.'[8]

It was possible that the passengers had been bluffing and would
have backed down as soon as the *Rainbow* dropped its gangplanks.
Burrell realized that Stevens and the immigration officials saw it
that way and thought he had given way unnecessarily, especially
on the question of the charter claim, but, in his own mind, he
had no doubt that his promise of an inquiry had been the turning-
point and had saved the government an extremely risky attempt
to take the ship by force.[9] The lawyers for the Indians thought
so as well. A. H. MacNeill wrote to the Prime Minister the
next day: 'It was very fortunate that the Honourable Mr Burrell
was in British Columbia, and arrived on the scene at the critical
moment. I can assure you that were it not for Mr Burrell's
presence here, no settlement could possibly have been arrived at.
The attitude of the local Immigration people and local politicians
was such as not to admit of any negotiations or settlement on any
terms. . . . I think that an investigation will disclose that there
never was any occasion for the night attack made by the immigration people on the *Komagata Maru*. The whole matter could have
been very readily avoided by the exercise of some slight degree of
diplomacy and consideration for the people who were on board,
as well as their friends on shore.'[10]

At about 1 a.m. eastern time, the Prime Minister learned the
outcome. Burrell had kept him posted by telegram at each stage
of the negotiations, and he had sent several telegrams to Vancouver, but the situation had not been one that he could manage
from Ottawa, and Borden had spent an apprehensive day. Around
suppertime in Ottawa—early afternoon in Vancouver—he had
received a telegram from Burrell containing the statement that
the guns of the *Rainbow* would not be used 'unless absolutely
necessary'. Alarmed, Borden replied: 'Cannot conceive that the
Rainbow guns could possibly become necessary. We agree that
control of the ship must be secured but we are opposed to so
extreme a measure.' Four-and-a-half hours later came Burrell's
explanation: there had been no intention of using the guns unless
the passengers were heavily armed, which was 'very improbable'.
The Prime Minister was aware, as Stevens and other local people
were not, of the imperial dimensions of the crisis. The Viceroy

of India had read a Reuter report that the Canadian government
intended to use military force, and he had warned the India Office
that this would have a 'very bad effect in India'. If it was a question of provisions, he added, 'it would be well worth while to
provide them'. His concern had been passed on to the Canadian
government by the Colonial Secretary: 'While vessel is in British
waters of course very desirable to avoid use of force which would
have extremely bad effect in Panjab.'[11] Borden knew that the eyes
of the British world were for the moment concentrated on Vancouver, and so it was with relief that he received the news that
everything had been worked out quietly. He did not question the
concessions that Burrell had made.

The passengers had allowed the crew into the engine room at
about 6.30 p.m., and that evening the immigration authorities
began sending out provisions. The militia were marched off and
dismissed at 8.30 p.m., and sometime after that the spectators
finally gave up hope of action and began to drift off home. Load-
ing continued through the morning and afternoon of the next
day, Wednesday, 22 July, as truck after truck of produce was
run out onto the wharf and transferred to the *Komagata Maru*
by the tug *Sea Lion*. Twenty tonnes of stove wood were ordered
and towed out in a scow. As word passed around that the ship
was indeed leaving, a large number of Indians came down to the
Immigration Office requesting permission to visit their friends on
board. Reid refused until late in the afternoon, when he agreed to
let them go in groups of ten for five minutes' conversation from
the deck of the immigration launch. Mitt Singh, the Secretary of
the Sikh Temple, had asked permission to take two women who
were friends of Kishen Kor, the only woman on the *Komagata
Maru*, but, when he brought them to the Immigration Office,
Reid found them looking suspiciously bulky, and, imagining that
they might be carrying weapons or ammunition, would not let
them go. In retaliation, when Mitt Singh and Rahim went out
with the fourth group of local Indians to visit the ship, they both
reached for the outstretched hands of passengers leaning over the
rail and jumped up onto the *Komagata Maru*. Reid considered
this a breach of faith and would have stopped all further visits,
but Hopkinson persuaded him to relent and was allowed to take
out another group of twelve.[12]

It was now about 6.30 p.m. The ship was due to sail with the early morning tide at 5 a.m. on Thursday the 23rd. The provisions were all on board, and the *Komagata Maru* appeared ready to slip away. However, Reid managed to manufacture another crisis. The Japanese Consul, Mr Hori, brought him a telegram from Bhag Singh, Rahim's co-charterer, now under detention in the United States where he had been held on petition from the Canadian authorities since he had been picked up with revolvers and ammunition on the 17th. Rahim had authorized the ship's departure in his own name and Bhag Singh's as well. Yet, here was a telegram from Bhag Singh declaring that he had not given his consent and that no one held power-of-attorney for him. The message had to be ignored, but it added to Reid's impatience. He did not trust the lawyer for the Indians and was afraid that they might go back on the settlement they had negotiated. He thought it imperative to get the ship out of the harbour ahead of the agreed time, an opinion that was reinforced within the half hour when Assistant Hindi Interpreter Henry Gwyther brought him a note from the passengers:

Sir: We have the honour to inform you that as the ship is ready to sail at 5 A.M. and we do not find some diet of eggs and meat in the provisions which is very necessary for us for so long a voyage; we request you to send some alive sheep, otherwise she could not be able to proceed tomorrow early in the morning. NOTE: Send three large brass prants [pots] for mixing up flour.

Reid had originally purchased about 1,150 kg. of canned salmon, but when the passengers objected to it, he had sent it back to the wholesalers without obtaining any substitute, expecting Sikhs to be content with a purely vegetarian diet. They had flour, potatoes, rice, pulse, cabbage, carrots, onions, butter, pickles, curry powder, ginger, sugar, salt, pepper, and tea, which he thought sufficient. This latest demand he interpreted, or chose to interpret, as another manoeuvre to delay departure, and he immediately got in touch with the militia officers and asked them again to call out their troops and to stand by at the C.P.R. detention shed. He was on his way to the *Rainbow* when he pulled alongside Hopkinson's launch and asked the Hindi Interpreter to come along with him to speak to Commander Hose. He said that he was not going to stand for any further parleying with these people and that he intended to give the *Komagata Maru* fifteen minutes to pull up anchor and get out. Force was to prevail. Hopkinson wanted no part of this and headed for shore to summon Burrell, Stevens, and the lawyers for both sides, having warned Reid to consult them before taking drastic action.[13]

During the day the large number of Indians collecting around the Immigration Office and on the dock had attracted crowds, but not on the scale of the day before when there had been greater promise of entertainment. By bringing out the militia in the evening, Reid recreated that promise. Rumours spread rapidly. It was reported in an evening paper that four of the Japanese crew had been thrown overboard, and that a Canadian pilot was being held prisoner, stories without any basis. Thousands of people came down to the waterfront on the heels of the 200 men of the Irish Fusiliers, the 72nd Highlanders, and the Duke of Connaught's Own Rifles. The militia were immediately set to work containing the crowds they had drawn themselves. As the numbers built up, the officials became more anxious and Burrell, feeling the pressure, became convinced that the public would not tolerate much more delay.

Reid, returning from the *Rainbow*, met Burrell, Stevens, Brigade Commander Duff Stuart, and Robie Reid who had been alerted by Hopkinson. It was agreed that the *Komagata Maru* should be given until 5 a.m., the time originally set, to weigh anchor, but if there was any hesitation after that, the *Rainbow* and militia should go into action. When A. H. MacNeill, the lawyer for the Indians, joined this conference he found the officials opposed to any further concessions, and believing that they were over-reacting, offered to buy the passengers what they wanted himself. At that hour—it was now about 11 p.m.—all that he could get were eggs, but he bought three cases and with members of the Shore Committee brought them out to the *Komagata Maru* at midnight. He came back to tell reporters that there was no trouble on the ship; the passengers did not appear aggressive, and, as far as he could see, they intended to leave as agreed. Some of them in fact had been helping the crew in the stokehold, and Captain Yamamoto had been surprised to learn of the alarm that had been engendered on shore.

The Shore Committee were allowed to stay on the *Komagata Maru* for the rest of the night. At 4 a.m., Hopkinson, who had had an hour or so of sleep in a bunk on the *Sea Lion*, came back to take them off. Some of the passengers were still throwing up wood from the scow, and the Hindi Interpreter warned them to hurry up if they wanted to have it on board by the time they left. It was a cold morning, and in the pre-dawn light the passengers worked fast. The last piece was thrown up just before 5 and on the hour the engines turned over. The men who had been working on the scow scrambled onto the deck of the steamer, and, at 5.10, only minutes after sunrise, she began to raise anchor. As the *Komagata Maru* pulled away, the passengers, leaning over the side, called out to the *Sea Lion* and some of them took off their sandals and boots and shook them. The gesture, Hopkinson explained, was intended for Malcolm Reid.

Early-morning spectators, and there were a large number spread along the shoreline above the C.P.R. docks, finally realized that there wasn't going to be any excitement when they saw the steamer disappear around Brockton Point as she headed into the narrows with the *Rainbow*, *Sea Lion*, and two launches behind her. Bhan Singh, who had asked for special permission to land, was expected to jump, and the *Sea Lion* trailed along ready to pull him from the water. He had claimed non-immigrant status as a student, a claim that Gurdit Singh disputed, figuring that Bhan Singh had given information and was getting consideration in exchange. To be sure of him, his fellow passengers had kept him below deck, handcuffing him at night, and, when the officials had collected Rughunath Singh, they had not attempted to take him as well.[14] He had been sending Reid desperate notes: 'They threaten to kill me on the way.' He would pay his own fare, he said, if he was allowed to get off the *Komagata Maru* and to take a C.P.R. boat: 'I don't want to spoil my life with this uneducated group of savages.' On the face of the envelope containing his last note, he had written 'I will jump as the ship departs as I want my life.'

The *Sea Lion* accompanied the *Komagata Maru* as far as Point Grey, a distance of ten or eleven kilometres. A life-buoy was held in readiness, and a photographer waited on top of the tug for Bhan Singh's great leap, but he never did appear. As the steamer left the inlet and entered the Strait of Georgia, the *Sea Lion* turned back while the *Rainbow* carried on for about 200 kilometres, through the Strait of Georgia, past the Gulf Islands, past the city of Victoria, and through the Strait of Juan de Fuca. In Plumpers Passage, within a few kilometres of Victoria, two

Japanese crewmen jumped from the *Komagata Maru* only to be picked up half-drowned by one of the cruiser's lifeboats.[15] When the two vessels reached international waters off Cape Flattery, they separated and the *Komagata Maru* ploughed out into the Pacific alone.

She was destined for Hong Kong by way of Yokohama. The passengers had tried to get the Canadian government to send them all the way to Calcutta but had been told that it was not possible. As the *Komagata Maru* steamed out of Vancouver, a telegram arrived in Ottawa from the Governor of Hong Kong who did not want the immigrants back and suggested that they be returned directly to India. 'It is certain', he stated, 'that there will be no employment for a large majority of the men here.' From Canada came the disingenuous reply that because the ship had sailed from Hong Kong, the Canadian government could not 'order the deportation of its passengers to any other point, nor compel the vessel to take them elsewhere'. Borden's government, ungrateful to Governor May for his warning in March of the imminent departure of the *Komagata Maru*, would not extend themselves to save him the embarrassment of her return.[16]

For the Canadian public, the affair was over, and readers turned to the editorial pages for some final comment. A number of Eastern Canadian papers were critical of official actions, particularly the use of the police on the early morning of the 19th, and there was a sharp attack on H. H. Stevens and the Borden government in the local opposition paper, the Vancouver *Sun*, which believed that a Liberal government would have settled the matter 'without resort to violence or threats or the display of force'. In his defence, Stevens was able to show letters from prominent Methodist and Presbyterian clergymen commending him for the part he had played.[17] Even the *Sun* conceded that, given the government's mismanagement, it had become necessary to call in the *Rainbow*. There was little reflection of MacNeill's opinion that 'some slight degree of diplomacy and consideration' would have been enough.

9

RETURN

On 16 August, after a rough crossing, the *Komagata Maru* reached Yokohama. While she had been at sea, Europe had gone to war. In Canadian newspapers, the developments in Europe had taken over the headlines, but for the Government of India, the war made the *Komagata Maru* more of a headache than ever.

Waiting at Yokohama was Sohon Singh Bhakna, founding member and first president of the *Ghadr* party, sent by his *Ghadr* friends from California with 200 automatic pistols and 2,000 rounds of ammunition expressly to meet the *Komagata Maru*. He had left San Francisco on 21 July and had arrived at Yokohama on 8 August. Daljit Singh and Harnam Singh Gujarawal came to his hotel and the next day he boarded the ship to explain *Ghadr* party plans to the passengers. With England at war, *Ghadr* leaders were beating the drum for recruits, saying that the moment had come, that this was the time to strike. At night the pistols were brought aboard and hidden with the help of one of the Japanese crew, the third engineer. Although the exact spot was a secret to all but a select few around Gurdit Singh, everyone on the ship knew what was going on.[1]

Also waiting for Gurdit Singh at Yokohama was a letter from the Colonial Secretary at Hong Kong threatening to arrest the passengers for vagrancy if they landed there. When Gurdit Singh wrote to the British Consul at Yokohama saying that his people were willing to go to any port in India if provisions were supplied, the Consul, with no instructions to guide him, refused to help.

The owners of the *Komagata Maru* ordered Captain Yamamoto to bring her to Kobe. She left Yokohama on the 18th and arrived at Kobe on the 21st. With the ship in Japanese waters, the owners wanted her back, Akira Nagata claiming 8,000 yen for coal purchased in Moji in April. The lights and water supply were cut off, and there was a change in the attitude of the crew as if to say that the voyage was now over and there was no more reason to be diplomatic. But the passengers were free to go ashore so their situation for the moment was not as uncomfortable as it had been during the worst days in Vancouver.[2]

Some passengers had left the ship at Yokohama, and another fifteen got off at Kobe. With them were two of Gurdit Singh's lieutenants, Bir Singh and Harnam Singh—not Harnam Singh Gujarawal—who had been given money to go to Shanghai and Hong Kong to collect men for the struggle in India.[3] Two men joined the ship. They were Sindhi students from Hyderabad, 23-year-old Jawahar Mal, a graduate in arts, and 17-year-old Narain Das, his brother. Jawahar Mal immediately took a lead in organizing processions of passengers and members of the small Indian community in Kobe. On successive days, they marched 150 strong around the town, Gurdit Singh riding a rickshaw loaded with garlands, ending up at the British Consulate, besieging Consul-General Forster who was impressed and perhaps intimidated. He invited the men in, and thirty filed through the entrance to the Consulate to be served tea. Forster considered their spokesman, Jawahar Mal, a very dangerous character. However, he sat down with the passengers and with Sato, the agent for the owners, and, as a result, wired the British Ambassador in Tokyo recommending assistance. The Ambassador authorized him to negotiate directly with the Government of India, and on 27 August he sent an urgent telegram.[4]

Sato had threatened to force the passengers off the ship in Kobe, although he admitted an obligation to provide transportation as far as Hong Kong, conceivably on another steamer. Consul Forster asked the Indian Government for 19,000 yen, enough to meet Nagata's claim for coal and to provision the *Komagata Maru* for the 20–5 day voyage to India.

Gurdit Singh wanted to buy the ship. Jawahar Mal had told the English-language press in Japan that the position of the passengers was so pitiable that they did not even have the means to telegraph India for help. That was propaganda. Gurdit Singh had money salted away, and since arriving in Japan, he had received more, thousands of dollars sent from Canada and the United States by his *Ghadr* friends.[5] That last night in Vancouver, when Husain Rahim, Mitt Singh, and other members of the Shore

Committee had been allowed to stay on the ship for several hours, they had agreed that they should try to buy her so that they could bring her from Calcutta according to Canadian law. They were not finished with the Canadian government and had not accepted defeat. In Kobe, Gurdit Singh made an offer and obtained a letter from Sato setting out terms of purchase. For this reason he was conserving every scrap of money he had.

The Indian government, going by Forster's telegram, had no choice, and authorized payment of up to 19,000 yen to bring the passengers home, as the Indian public would have reacted strongly if the men on the *Komagata Maru* had been left stranded in Japan. Nine thousand yen were handed directly to the passengers for provisions, and on Wednesday, 2 September, they made ready to sail. While still within sight of shore, they discovered that, on instructions from India, they were bound for Madras, not Calcutta. About three kilometres out they forced the crew to drop anchor, and only after the clearance papers were changed did they agree to go on. The *Komagata Maru* finally left Kobe on Thursday, 3 September.

On 8 September, the Viceroy, Lord Hardinge, addressed his Legislative Council at the opening of a new session at Simla, the capital during the hot season. He spoke about the war and about the *Komagata Maru*. He had offered the King 'the finest and largest military force of British and Indian troops' that had ever left the shores of India, and he asked Indians to show the world 'an attitude of unity, of self-sacrifice and of unswerving confidence under all circumstances in the justice of our cause and in the assurance that God will defend the right.' The recent history of the *Komagata Maru* was an embarrassment that he tried to dismiss, denying that India had a grievance against any of the Dominions or that there was a policy of exclusion directed against Indians alone, claiming, incorrectly, that Canada had an ordinance in force that kept out all labourers, even from the United Kingdom. He told the Council that everyone should regret the discomfort suffered by the passengers of the *Komagata Maru*, but, he said, the organizers of the voyage were 'culpably responsible' because 'They must have known perfectly well that entry would be refused. . . .'[6]

Lord Hardinge was speaking to a body made up of thirty-eight officials and nominees, mostly European, and twenty-seven elected members, nearly all Indian. (The inclusion of the latter had been an innovation only five years earlier.) Surendra Nath Banerjea of Bengal and Khan Bahadur Mir Asad Ali Khan, representing the Mohammedan community of Madras, wanted to know what the Indian government had done about the treatment of the passengers of the *Komagata Maru* and what it proposed to do to gain better treatment for Indian emigrants in the future. The answers they got were not very enlightening. The Viceroy had taken the position that, as long as the passengers' case had been before the Canadian courts, his government had no reason to intervene. When the Canadians were considering the use of armed force, he had made representations, and, he pointed out, no force had been used. That was all that he or his officials were willing to say.

There was one aspect of the situation that Hardinge did not want to make public since it would serve only to advertise dissension. He knew, thanks to Hopkinson, that the revolutionaries in North America were at work organizing a mass return to raise the banner of revolt. Days after Britain's declaration of war, there had been meetings at Fresno, Stockton, and Sacramento, California, and at Portland, Oregon, to recruit men and money for the cause. Hopkinson had reported on this activity by 11 August, and, subsequently, he had identified twenty-six seditionists leaving Victoria, 22 August, by the C.P.R. *Empress of India*, nineteen from Vancouver, 25 August, by *Shidzukoa Maru*, and sixty-three from San Francisco, 29 August, by the Pacific Mail Steamship Co. *Korea*. Forewarned, the Viceroy, by special ordinance, had assumed the power to arrest anyone entering the country if it was judged necessary to protect the safety, interest, or tranquillity of the state. This was the Ingress to India Ordinance which had become law on 5 September.[7]

When the *Komagata Maru* was in Kobe, the Indian government had asked Consul-General Forster to telegraph the names of troublemakers. (The only one he supplied was that of Jawahar Mal.) Some thought was given to sending officers to Singapore to travel the rest of the way on board the ship, but, apparently, there had not been enough time. Nevertheless, when the *Komagata Maru* reached Singapore on 16 September, she was a marked ship and the officials there refused to allow any of her passengers ashore. There were a number of men who wanted to disembark, some hoping to find employment and the Sindhi brothers, Jawahar

Mal and Narain Das, intending to change ships for Bombay. The closest that they got to port was an anchorage five kilometres out in the straits. Gurdit Singh wanted to land to purchase provisions but was not given permission even though he had been a longtime resident of the Malay States and had come and gone freely in the past. After two or three days, the passengers decided that there was nothing to be gained by further delay—the Singapore authorities were not going to back down—and on 19 September the *Komagata Maru* began the last leg of her voyage.[8]

While the *Komagata Maru* passed through the Strait of Malacca and crossed the Andaman Sea and the Bay of Bengal, the compact German cruiser *Emden* was on the prowl, first appearing near the mouth of the Hooghly River to sink five steamers coming down from Calcutta on the 15th, and then, during the following two weeks, roaming in the Bay of Bengal, sinking a sixth vessel, approaching close to Rangoon, shelling Madras, and passing openly within sight of Pondicherry. Three British cruisers had been unable to catch up with her, and she had been seen boldly coaling by night with powerful lights that showed her up for miles. Shipping in and out of the port of Calcutta was much reduced, and, as a consequence, large numbers of casual labourers on the docks went unemployed, an emergency that the District Charitable Society tried to meet by voluntary subscriptions for the purchase of food.[9]

The state of war, unemployment in Calcutta, and the suspected *Ghadr* connection with the ship were all the excuse that the Indian authorities needed to use the new Ingress to India Ordinance against the passengers of the *Komagata Maru*. In consultation with the Government of the Panjab and the Government of India, the local Government of Bengal decided to take the passengers off at Budge Budge, before they reached Calcutta, and to transport most of them by train at government expense to their homes in the Panjab, arresting and detaining any who appeared to be agitators. A party of Panjab police was sent to Calcutta to be on hand when the ship arrived.[10]

At high tide on the evening of Saturday, 26 September, the *Komagata Maru* entered the mouth of the Hooghly. She was running at a good speed when she came opposite Kalpi, a small village on the east bank, about ninety kilometres downstream from Calcutta. A European officer in a launch signalled, and the steamer drifted to a stop, anchoring well out from shore. Local people in small boats tried to approach to sell goods but were waved off by the pilot. The passengers themselves were not allowed to go ashore.

On Sunday morning, the ship had three high-ranking visitors: James Donald, magistrate and chief administrative officer of the surrounding district, 24-Parganas, F. S. A. Slocock from the office of the Director of Criminal Intelligence for the Government of India, and R. Humphreys, a Deputy Commissioner from Hoshiarpur District in the Panjab. These men were accompanied by a number of Panjabi constables, a Panjabi Deputy Superintendent, Sukha Singh, and two European Panjab police officers. The police were not in uniform, and, for a moment, Gurdit Singh thought they were friends. He had hoped that a delegation of Indian spokesmen would meet the ship to publicize the grievances of its passengers, but the telegrams he had tried to send from Singapore had apparently not been received. Instead, he had the police looking for arms and for copies of the *Ghadr* in the cabins, the steerage area, and the luggage. The revolvers that had been acquired at Yokohama were safely hidden, although some had rusted because, wrapped in sheets, they had been put in the water instead of the oil tank. The police were half-convinced when Gurdit Singh told them that, after Singapore, he had discovered revolvers purchased from the Japanese crew by some of the passengers, and had ordered the weapons thrown overboard.[11]

They returned on Monday to ferret through the luggage again and to search some of the passengers, but they found nothing and the *Komagata Maru* was allowed to proceed slowly up the Hooghly towards Calcutta.

It was late Tuesday morning, 29 September, when the *Komagata Maru* approached the industrial town of Budge Budge, about sixty-five kilometres up the Hooghly from Kalpi and roughly twenty-seven kilometres by river from Calcutta. A launch carrying the same officials who had been at Kalpi drew alongside, and at 11 a.m. these men stepped on board. With them was Sir Frederick Halliday, the Commissioner of Police for Calcutta. The *Komagata Maru* reduced speed and a few minutes later tied up at a floating jetty near the Budge Budge railway station. Deputy Commissioner Humphreys called Gurdit Singh to the Captain's cabin and for the first time explained that this was where the passengers had to get off to take a special train to the Panjab. Gurdit Singh refused. He had reason to be suspicious because Budge Budge was on the wrong side of the river and there were no railway bridges at Calcutta or below.[12]

Two railway stations served Calcutta. Howrah, on the far side, was the station for the then United Provinces and the Panjab, and Sealdah, on the Budge Budge side, took one to eastern Bengal and Assam. The special train now sitting a few hundred yards from the *Komagata Maru* was to run through the southern and eastern parts of Calcutta, past Sealdah station, and north along the Hooghly for forty kilometres to cross by the railway bridge at Naihati. For the authorities it was easier to use this roundabout routing than to cope with a disembarkation in Calcutta. But Gurdit Singh would not concede that there was a bridge at Naihati, and, when Humphreys suggested that a deputation of passengers go to the station to look at a timetable, he still objected because, as he explained, he had personal business connected with the *Komagata Maru* that could not be adjusted unless he went in person before an arbitrator in Calcutta.

Gurdit Singh turned to Jawahar Mal and the members of the passengers committee who had been standing outside the cabin door and fell into urgent conversation. The officials, moving freely among the other passengers, were approached quietly by seventeen Muslims from the Shahpur district who claimed that they had been bullied by Gurdit Singh and his gang of Sikhs and robbed of all their money—one made a motion indicating he was afraid his throat would be cut—and said they wanted to disembark. With Bhan Singh's help, the Captain lowered the gangway and the Muslims got down onto the landing pontoon with their luggage. Halliday and Slocock took them through the yard of the Indo-Burma Oil Company to the railway station, a distance of less than half a kilometre, and put them on the train. In the meantime many of the Sikhs had been persuaded to disembark and when Slocock and Halliday returned from the station they saw that a large number had their boxes and bundles on the pontoon but were refusing to step ashore until Gurdit Singh left the ship. The police—twenty-seven Panjabi constables carrying swords but not firearms—were not able to force the issue and the officials waited for the passengers to move of their own accord. After some delay, the last twenty or thirty passengers came down the gangway with Gurdit Singh carrying the Holy Book, the *Granth Sahib*, on his head. The whole body of Sikhs formed a procession and marched as far as a large tree near a level crossing forty yards from the railway platform. There they sat down. They would not carry their own luggage which they had left on the pontoon, saying that was a job for coolies. It was a holiday and there were not many coolies around, but Slocock found a few and they began bringing up the luggage.[13]

The officials had assumed that only a few passengers were attached to Gurdit Singh and that the majority would not be a problem. But a problem they now were. Donald decided to give a formal warning, and he produced a copy of the Ingress to India Ordinance which he read out in English, a language which few of the passengers understood fully but which their leaders knew well enough. All he got was argument. Gurdit Singh charged the Government with duplicity: the train could not be going to the Panjab; it must be going to Assam; it was on that side of the river. He said that the passengers wanted to go to Calcutta for work because there was no work in Panjab at that time of year. In any case, he said, they could not leave without a chance to arrange their affairs. A number owed him money, and there were 533 bedsteads and other articles that had not been removed from the ship. They needed a lawyer, and it would take a week to straighten everything out. And, he added, it would be sacrilegious to take the *Granth Sahib* on the train. They would have to take it to Howrah to the *gurdwara* there.[14]

The officials were imperious, the passengers agitated and threatening. Halliday and Donald went to the telegraph office to phone Sir William Duke, the only member of the Executive Council of Bengal who could be reached at the time. They wanted troops, but it was difficult for Duke to sanction force when he knew that Canada had earlier been warned against it. He promised to put troops on the alert, but was not convinced they were needed. Go back, were his instructions, and try to persuade the Sikhs onto the train.

It was about 3 in the afternoon when Halliday and Donald walked back along the track to the level crossing. Some time between 3 and 4 p.m., the Sikhs stood up and, instead of making their way along the path to the station, crossed the railway line. The police could not stop them, although they persuaded forty-five to turn back and board the train. The rest, 250 strong, carried on down the road towards Calcutta. The police, under Deputy Superintendent Sukha Singh, followed with instructions to stay close behind but not to get in the way. Donald phoned the Chief Secretary to the Government of Bengal, and, between 4 and 5 p.m., 150 Royal Fusiliers of the City of London Regiment were dispatched in motor-cars from Fort William in Calcutta. Halliday called police headquarters in Calcutta, and Superintendent J. H. Eastwood of the Reserve Police, a fifty-year-old veteran of the Nile expedition and the South African war, quickly collected thirty European sergeants and constables and brought them along the road to Budge Budge.[15] They rode in whatever transport they could find immediately, a prison van, a fire engine, and several taxi cabs.

Halliday, Donald, and Slocock set out by motor-car to meet the Fusiliers, but when they overtook the Sikhs about three kilometres outside the town, they decided it would be dangerous to try to go through. They drove back to Budge Budge and took the train—with those who had boarded it willingly—to Majer Hat, a station on a branch line south of Calcutta, well away from trouble.

Six or seven kilometres along the road from Budge Budge, the Sikhs encountered Superintendent Eastwood and his small police force. They tried to push past, but the police—five carrying revolvers and the rest with bamboo sticks—held their ground until the Royal Fusiliers came up. With the troops were J. G. Cumming, Chief Secretary to the Government of Bengal, and Sir William Duke. Duke drove up to Gurdit Singh and asked where he and his followers were going.

'We are going to Calcutta.'

'What business have you in Calcutta?'

'First to deposit the Holy Book in a Gurdwara and afterwards to seek an interview with the Governor before whom we will lay our grievances.'

'The Governor has sent me to hear your case. I am his Commissioner.'

'If such is the case, very well listen to me. I will relate you the miseries and injustices suffered by us.'

'Not here. Return with me to the Budge Budge station where I would hear your case.'[16]

This was not a reassuring promise, but ahead, along the highway, was a convoy of troops armed with .303 rifles. Without any certainty about their ultimate destination, the Sikhs turned around. The Panjab and European police accompanied them on foot, while the troops followed at a distance in their motor–cars.

In this fashion, the procession moved at a steady pace, covering about five kilometres in an hour. Gurdit Singh rode along on a bicycle purchased from a Bengali boy met on the way. It had been a hot afternoon, and many of the Sikhs tried to slip into shops or bye-ways along the route to get water, but the European police sergeants chased after them and pushed them back into the ranks with a kick or two. Otherwise, the Sikhs went quietly, and when Halliday came up from behind in a motor-car, returning from Majer Hat, he drove through them without any incident.

The sun had set while they were some distance from Budge Budge. As they approached the station a little before 7 p.m., it was becoming dark with the moon rising in the sky behind them. Sir William Duke had gone ahead to secure a train and it was standing at the station platform. However, as the police arrived at the level crossing, they were not sure whether the train was ready or whether the Sikhs should be taken back to the *Komagata Maru* for the night. A halt was called, and the Sikhs were told to sit down and wait on a grass plot just west of the railway line. A few metres back was a ditch or pond in which the water level lay about two metres below the road surface. Immediately in front was a one-and-a-half metre corrugated-iron fence, with spikes, which ran along the railway line. On one side, a path led between the ditch and the fence to the station platform. On the other side was the road to the landing pontoon where they had disembarked that afternoon.

Sir Frederick Halliday positioned the Panjab police in a single line to the right of the Sikhs to prevent them from breaking away again towards Calcutta. The European police formed a line on the other side of the crowd. As the Sikhs began to sit down around the *Granth Sahib* which they had carried with them on a portable platform, Halliday walked up to the level crossing in search of Sir William Duke who was, in fact, still in the station building. Halliday had not been at the crossing for more than a minute when there was the crackle of a series of explosions on the far side of the crowd. The Sikhs had jumped to their feet. The explosions were revolver shots and Halliday could hear the whine of bullets over his head.[17]

Donald, the District Magistrate, had approached the crowd from the station side to summon Gurdit Singh. The old man had refused to come near, saying that Donald could speak to him where he was. A European police sergeant starting in after him had been called back, but Superintendent Eastwood had plunged in among the Sikhs, possibly to get a bamboo stick snatched from one of his men, or, more likely, to get Gurdit Singh. He had taken a few steps when the crowd had closed in on him and he had been knocked to the ground. At that moment the firing had begun.

Later when asked to explain what had happened, Halliday said he had seen thirty or forty Sikhs, spotted throughout the crowd, all firing. It was an impression that some of his own officers did not share and it may well have been exaggerated. Some of the shots came from four police sergeants, now engulfed by the crowd and discharging their revolvers at such close quarters that one man, Badal Singh, was hit six times. But the rest came from the passengers, striking Malcolm Lomax, Assistant Traffic Superintendent for the East Bengal Railway, in the abdomen, catching David Petrie, one of the European officers with the Panjab police, in the arm and thigh, and grazing Deputy Commissioner Humphreys on the forehead. As the passengers surged forward, the Calcutta police and the Panjabi constables struck back with bamboo *lathis* and with swords. A blow by a stick broke Sub-Inspector Nanak Chand's left arm while Constable Hari Singh had the bone of the same arm severed by some sharp instrument and took a six-inch head wound which exposed the brain. The police were driven back, although not before some of them reached Eastwood who had received a bullet in the back, and dragged him from the spot where he had slumped.

The Royal Fusiliers had entered Budge Budge behind everyone else and were a long way down the road on the far side of the track when the first shots were fired. Two platoons came up on the double and established themselves behind the iron fence along the railway right of way. From their side of the fence, in failing light, they had only a limited view of the action. The commanding officer, Captain Francis Moore, waited a matter of minutes or seconds while the police extracted themselves, some seeking refuge in the station, others making for the level crossing. Moore approached Sir Frederick Halliday, still standing at the level crossing, and asked if he should give the order to fire. Halliday said yes, only a moment before he, himself, was wounded in the foot.

When the troops opened fire, most of the passengers found shelter in the ditch behind them. Some ran towards a *modie's* or grocer's about fifteen metres from the railway. Others hid behind a watchman's hut at the level crossing, and the trunk of a large tree nearby, from where there was still some shooting, and the troops concentrated their fire at them. The riots had begun about 7 p.m. Within an hour, almost all the passengers had worked their way along the ditch and had slipped off in the darkness in the direction of the oil tanks and the river beyond. At 8, a number emerged at a run from behind the watchman's hut and the shops and escaped into the night. The troops fired a volley after them and all was quiet.

8

IO

ARREST AND DETENTION

Among the wounded discovered in the shadows when the firing ended were eight passengers from the *Komagata Maru* and a Bengali spectator. They were taken to Medical College Hospital in Calcutta. Two of the passengers, shot in the stomach, died on the way and after they were examined by the resident surgeon, went nameless to the morgue. Twenty-five passengers were captured that night, but the rest were unaccounted for. Captain Moore set out pickets around the railway station, rounded up all the European women and children in the area, and put them into a house guarded by some of his troops. About half an hour after the shooting was over, a Panjabi constable, searching a plot of ground at the back of the station, sword in hand, was mistaken for a runaway Sikh, fired at by two soldiers, and fatally injured.

By daylight the next morning the bodies of twelve Sikhs were collected in the vicinity of the station. A journalist who came down from Calcutta on Wednesday afternoon, found them laid out in a line in preparation for removal. He noted dispassionately that they appeared to have been well fed. The morning light also showed the bodies of two local people. Rukmini Kanta Majumder, a relative of the compound keeper of the local hospital, had been hit by the rifle fire of the troops as he came up from the river in the dark. Dinabandu Pande was found in his master's shop, his stomach slashed open by a knife or sword.[1]

A massive search was organized in the vicinity of Budge Budge and the countryside beyond. Local villagers had seen some of the Sikhs hiding in paddy fields, lying in water up to their necks, or crouching in high grass and vegetation. They reported that a good number had crossed the river in a couple of boats. Only forty-six or forty-eight were found that day, most of them within a few kilometres of Budge Budge, although one was picked up at Behala and another at Garden Reach on the southern and western out-skirts of Calcutta. Among the arrested was little Balwant Singh, Gurdit Singh's seven-year-old son, who had been abandoned by his father during the riot.

Gurdit Singh had spent several hours partially submerged in a pool. Just before dawn, he had broken into a bungalow not far from the railway station. The owners would not shelter him, but gave him a clean *dhoti* and kerchief, took him to the river, and spoke to the ferryman. The old man paid a rupee for an eight-anna fare and was given a covered seat on the boat. In this way he had gained the other side of the Hooghly, and by 10 p.m. he had managed to slip onto a train for Puri (Jagannathdham) on the Bay of Bengal, a night and a day's journey to the south-west.[2]

Few of the passengers were as resourceful as he was, neither as worldly nor as well-provided with rupees. As darkness fell on Wednesday night, some stole out of hiding places within one to one and-a-half kilometres of Budge Budge, seeking food and clothing. Their manner, according to the local villagers, was not at all aggressive; rather, they appeared terror-stricken and delirious from hunger and exposure. Their dress, their beards, their hair and their speech all marked them as foreign to Bengal. Some offered gold coins for Bengali clothing, but the local people were reluctant to risk anything for them.[3]

On Wednesday, the Government of Bengal issued a statement claiming that the passengers had fired first and without warning.[4] The statement concluded:

The Government of Bengal deeply deplore the loss of life which has occurred. They were acting in pursuance of the openly declared intention of sending to their homes the passengers who had suffered so much in pocket by the voyages of this ship. They were aware of the existence of a certain amount of political discontent amongst some of the passengers; and in full concurrence with the Punjab Government, considered that their return to their native country should be prompt and direct. Needless to say, no one had the smallest suspicion that any of the party were armed for a desperate attack on British officers.

At the time this statement was given out, about 170 of the passengers remained at large. Sixteen were known to be dead as well as two Bengalis, a Panjabi constable, and Lomax, the railway official. Superintendent Eastwood was in a critical condition at Presidency General Hospital, and the wounded who had been taken to Medical College Hospital were all in bad shape. On Thursday morning, the body of a Sikh was found floating in the river. He had been shot in the head and had apparently staggered into the water and drowned. At noon, one of the wounded at the Medical College Hospital died, bringing the death toll among the passengers to eighteen.[5]

The more fortunate men, those who had left by train a couple of hours before the riot, arrived at Ludhiana in the Panjab on Friday, 2 October. They had come through at high speed, stopping only at Naihati—where they were given a snack on the first evening, Allahabad—where they all got off and refused to reembark until they were fed again, and Delhi. They had been accompanied by a single police officer, but when they arrived at Ludhiana, they saw the station area jammed with Panjabi police guards who had been told they were German spies. They were kept on the train for the night and then taken to Ludhiana municipal hall where they were held for a week and interrogated separately. Most of them gave short statements, loyal to Gurdit Singh, but they knew that two of their number, Bhan Singh, the student, and Polo Ram, his friend, were talking at length. At the end of the week, they were sent to their villages, the government paying their fares.[6]

During the second day of searches in and around Budge Budge, the authorities found the only woman from the *Komagata Maru*, Kishen Kor, hiding with her husband, Sundar Singh, and their two children, the youngest little more than an infant. She was sent with the children by train to the Panjab, while he was arrested and taken to jail. The Calcutta and Bengal police were stopping any Sikh who could not explain who he was and where he had come from, keeping a special watch on the Howrah and Sealdah stations. Rewards of 100 rupees for each arrest were proclaimed by drum beat in the districts where the fugitives were known to be hiding, and, for several days after the riot, patrols swept not just the immediate vicinity of Budge Budge, but an area with a fifteen to twenty-five kilometre radius. One Harnam Singh, found on Thursday, 2 October, cowering in an *arahar* field close to Budge Budge, was typical of the state of many passengers. Yet, on the same day, police were told that eighty Sikhs had marched in two batches along the road from Chanditala to Sheakhala, thirty kilometres north-west of Calcutta. That night, a special force of fifty troops caught up with twenty-five of them sleeping in a meadow surrounded by irrigation tanks. According to the troops, the Sikhs answered a warning shot with revolver fire and tried to escape, but seventeen of them were arrested immediately and two more a few kilometres down the road. By the end of the week, there were only eighty-five fugitives uncaught. For a few more days, police continued to pick up *Komagata Maru* men on the outskirts of Calcutta and in the 24-Parganas, but, on 8 October, five were arrested at Midnapore, 100 kilometres west of Calcutta, and, four days later, nineteen were taken at Bankura, even further to the north-west. After that, police efforts were less fruitful, although the government was intent on bringing in the forty-odd passengers who were still free.[7]

Over 2,000 people attended the full-dress military funeral for Superintendent Eastwood who had rallied briefly but had died of internal hemorrhaging on the morning of Saturday, 3 October. It occurred to no one in the British Community in India that the fault might lie with the government, and in the face of this attitude, the conservative Sikh leadership showed no courage. On 6 October, a meeting of Sikhs at the Golden Temple of Amritsar disowned the actions of the passengers of the *Komagata Maru* and declared unflinching loyalty to the British crown. On 8 October, at the Burrabazar Sikh Temple, a similar meeting of Sikh and Panjabi residents of Calcutta condemned the violence of the passengers and expressed sympathy with the families of police officers and others who had been killed and wounded. Those who attended wished to contradict rumours and to blunt the political implications of the incident. It was, one speaker declared, 'purely and simply an isolated local affair. . . . These simple folk misunderstood the beneficent intention of their Government and hence the row. However heinous at first their offence appeared to be, it was the work of neither anarchists nor cut-throats. It was the result of misunderstanding, purely and simply.' He hoped it would be taken in that light and treated as such.[8]

Most Indian journalists were inhibited by knowledge of police powers under the Press Act and with reason, because two Punjabi language papers, *Khalsa Akhbar* and *Shere Punjab*, were shut down after publishing strongly-worded articles. However, Surendra Nath Banerjea, the moderate voice of Bengal, began calling for a formal inquiry from the moment that the Bengal Government's statement first appeared. One of a series of editorials in his paper, *The Bengali*, put the issue this way:[9]

> We think that the authorities should explain why they felt it necessary to compel the Sikh immigrants to proceed to their homes and to prevent them from going to Calcutta as some of them apparently wanted. Such a proceeding could only be justified in the interests of law and order and the maintenance of public tranquillity. The authorities had undoubtedly their reasons, and they probably acted upon Police reports, but we know that these reports are not always gospel truth. We really do not think that any serious danger was likely to happen from their being allowed to go to Calcutta....Deplorable as the incident is, we feel that with tact and judgement it might have been avoided.

Calcutta's coroner was investigating the deaths of Malcolm Lomax and three unnamed Sikhs who had been taken to Medical College Hospital on the evening of the riot—the first deaths reported to him. On the morning of the second day following the riot, he had taken a jury to view the bodies in the morgue, an occasion which attracted a large crowd on Colootollah St. where the morgue was situated. Two weeks later, the jury heard evidence. The principal witness, Police Commissioner Sir Frederick Halliday, had not seen the first shots fired, and the three police sergeants questioned were those who had helped bring the wounded to hospital. Only one had been present when the firing took place, and he was not certain what had happened. 'I cannot say who fired the first shot.' The testimony of the police surgeon who had conducted the post-mortem examinations and of the resident surgeon of the Medical College Hospital, established nothing except the weight of the bullet found in Lomax. However, in charging the jury, the coroner declared that the police and troops had had no alternative but to fire and that 'absolutely no provocation had been given to the Sikhs.'[10]

A nineteenth passenger, Tehal Singh, died—of cholera—at Medical College Hospital on the morning of 13 October. In the Panjab, a number of meetings held amongst Sikhs sympathetic to the passengers produced petitions to Lord Hardinge denouncing the accounts given in the English-language papers, rejecting the statement of the Bengal Government, and calling for an impartial inquiry. This campaign, supported by Surendra Nath Banerjea's moderate following in the Bengal-based Indian Association, persuaded Hardinge that an inquiry was necessary, if only to protect his image as a sympathetic Viceroy. On 15 October, the Government of India announced the appointment of a committee to report not only on the Budge Budge incident, but on the whole history of the *Komagata Maru*.

The Committee was not a strong one and that did not escape notice. It was made up of three officials and two non-officials and the latter, Sardar Daljit Singh, the great-uncle of the Maharajah of Kapurthala, and Sir Bijoy Chand Mahtab, the Maharajadhiraj of Burdwan, were not known for their independence. Yet Surendra Nath Banerjea was exultant because the Viceroy had responded to public pressure so soon after the event. 'We can only hope', he wrote in *The Bengali*, 'that the Committee imbued with the spirit of firmness and justice seasoned with mercy which has marked the conduct of His Excellency in this connection will address themselves to their work with an open mind and restore by their labours the confidence of the public in his unmistakably beneficent policy.'[11]

The Committee convened on Friday, 23 October, at the old Government of India Legislative Department behind Calcutta's Town Hall, and meeting daily behind closed doors, finished its work in six weeks. There was a trip to Budge Budge to visit the *Komagata Maru* and to look over the scene of the riot, and some meetings were held in Jullunder in the Panjab to hear evidence from passengers who had boarded the train and who were now at home. As the Committee began its work, 193 passengers were under detention, most of them at the Kalighat Jail in Calcutta; another eight or nine were in the care of the Medical College Hospital; during the last days of October, ten more were arrested. All of them were kept prisoners until the inquiry was over. Gurdit Singh, in flight, with a reward of 1,000 rupees promised for his arrest, had reached the eastern regions of Hyderabad. He wanted to tell his story and sent a messenger north to Amritsar with letters for the Sikh papers, *Khalsa Samachar*, *Khalsa Sewak*, and others. Two weeks later, the messenger returned with the news that his small son, Balwant, had not yet arrived home and was perhaps in jail. He was being held in the Kalighat Jail at the pleasure of the Committee.[12]

Nearly 1,000 printed pages of evidence were amassed by the Committee and none made public. They had testimony from the unfortunate Captain Yamamoto, Chief Engineer Shiozaki, and

Chief Officer Miaji, still waiting in Calcutta for the release of their ship; from Magistrate Donald and other officials and police officers; from the station master, Indian railway officials, and local residents of Budge Budge; at Jullunder, from some of the passengers who had been returned home, in particular Polo Ram and Bhan Singh, willing now as in Vancouver to speak damagingly of Gurdit Singh; and finally from the prisoners themselves.[13] The Committee's central witness was still on the loose. 'We think it only fair to Gurdit Singh', the Committee noted in their Report, 'to observe that we had not had his version of the facts.' But they did have several account books and a history of the voyage prepared by Gurdit Singh and found among his documents in the cabin after the riot.

The prisoners said they had been unarmed and that the police had fired without reason. It was impossible for the police to say which of them had done the actual shooting; and the inquiry led to no prosecutions. However, several American revolvers—Smith & Wesson .38 calibre with similar serial numbers and clearly of common origin—had been found at Budge Budge, and Surain Singh, a passenger from Gurdit Singh's own village of Sirhali, had been captured with a Smith & Wesson in his possession. He had been separated from the rest, taken to Midnapur Central Jail, and he had testified that Gurdit Singh had handed him the revolver and forty-six cartridges just before they landed. Another man from Sirhali, Mana Singh, not a passenger on the *Komagata Maru*, but an emigrant recently returned from America and arrested burgling a house in Lyallpur in late October, told the police about revolvers acquired in Japan. Captain Yamamoto admitted some knowledge: 'Some of Bhan Singh's followers told me at Yokohama that two or three boxes full of automatic revolvers had been brought on board during the night. I did not see the boxes myself.'[14] Chief Engineer Shiozaki, Bhan Singh, Polo Ram, and one of the wounded at Medical College Hospital, Pir Baksh, said there had been revolvers on board, but their stories varied, and the Committee could only guess at the truth.

As the inquiry drew to a close, ninety-two prisoners were sent home, leaving Howrah station by the Delhi Express in four groups on the 1st, 2nd, 3rd, and 4th of December.[15] Once they reached their villages, their movements were restricted by official order. Nor was the search relaxed for the passengers who had so

far evaded arrest. In mid-December, one of the latter, Sadha
Singh of Chukarchak village, Ferozepore district, was captured
after finding his way back to the Panjab. He gave the police a
statement saying that Gurdit Singh had armed the passengers.
'We arrived at Budge Budge and were landed at noon', Sadha
Singh testified. '[Deputy] Superintendent Sukha Singh and the
police landed and then Gurdit Singh got the boxes of pistols and
distributed them among his friends.'[16]

The Inquiry Committee Report was released when the Legislative Council of India re-assembled during the second week of
January 1915. As one should have expected, the Committee backed
officialdom all the way. Canada and the Canadian authorities escaped censure, and the police at Budge Budge were criticized
only for searching the ship less carefully than circumstances
required. At the same time, the revolutionary character of the
ship was played down, the Committee providing sedition no more
publicity than necessary. They gave Gurdit Singh no credit for
political conviction, but the motive of money. Their report boiled
down to this: in the pursuit of profit, Gurdit Singh had defrauded
men, telling them they could land in Vancouver when the law
barred the way, and, when the ship had been turned back, stirred
up anti-government feelings to cover up his own misdeeds. Then
he had purchased revolvers to act out the part of a revolutionary,
and, fearing arrest, had given them to his friends on the 29th to
use if the police made a move against him. All the blame was his.

A less partial jury might have noted that while some of the
passengers were carrying arms, Budge Budge was not the place
to use them, especially after the police had been reinforced by
troops, and that if the passengers had fired first it must have been
under provocation and without calculation.

Eighty-seven passengers were sent home from prison in the
latter part of January. Almost nine months had passed since the
Komagata Maru had sailed from Yokohama with 376. One had
died in hospital shortly after arriving in Vancouver. Twenty
returning residents had been landed in Canada, and Rughunath
Singh, his wife and son, had been taken off the ship a few days
before it started back. Thirty-three had disembarked in Japan and
the two Sindhi brothers had got on. At Budge Budge, fifty-nine
had boarded the train for Ludhiana, and Kishen Kor and her two
children had been sent on afterwards. Following the riot, twenty

died—the total had risen once more—and twenty-seven were fugitives, among them Gurdit Singh and his Secretary, Daljit Singh. Two men had managed to get back to the Panjab before being arrested and briefly detained, and now 179 had been released from jail in Calcutta. Thirty-one remained prisoners. They included members of the passengers committee, Amir Mohammed Khan, Amar Singh Nihang, Harnam Singh of Khabra, Sundar Singh of Ajitwal, and others close to Gurdit Singh.[17]

There was little sign that anyone, outside a comparatively small cadre of revolutionaries, cared about these men. It was not simply a question of a muffled press. Indian leaders were supporting the British war effort in the belief that loyalty would be rewarded by steps towards self-government. Gandhi, the hero of the satyagraha campaign in South Africa, had offered his services to the British Secretary of State and had helped to raise a volunteer ambulance corps. Moderates, still in control of the All-India Congress, were vigorously protesting their loyalty, and even the so-called extremist B. G. Tilak had emerged from prison in August 1914, condemning revolutionary acts of violence. The treatment that the passengers of the *Komagata Maru* had received in Canada was something that all Indians could deplore, but the use of arms was another matter, and here the Inquiry Committee *Report*—however imperfect—served its purpose because, on the evidence available, there did not seem to be any challenge to the conclusion that the passengers had been armed and had attacked the police.

It disgusted Gurdit Singh, hiding in Karimnagar, Hyderabad, and at work on his own account of the affair, to read in Gurmukhi papers from Amritsar that Sikh leaders had dissociated themselves from the rioters at Budge Budge and were advising their people that they should not take part in any political or anti-government activity. He could not answer back: letters he sent to the papers were not published. Only in subversive publications smuggled in from North America might one learn that there was another side to the story of the *Komagata Maru*.[18]

During the autumn and spring of 1914–15, several thousand Sikhs had returned to India from Canada and the United States. 'Go to your country and set up a rebellion at once', they had been told. 'Your enemy is in difficulties. . . . He is hemmed in by the German lion.'[19] The government, warned by Hopkinson, had been prepared when an advance guard of the most dedicated revolutionaries from Victoria, Vancouver, and San Francisco had arrived at Calcutta on 29 October among the passengers of the *Tosha Maru*. They had been met at Kidderpore docks by Police Commissioner Halliday with two companies of Royal Fusiliers, a special detachment of 200 armed European and Indian police from Dacca, and 500 or 600 Indian troops from the Panjab.[20] Revolvers had been found in the possession of two passengers and seditious leaflets in the baggage of ten others. The remainder had been embarked by train that night for Ludhiana where the Panjab authorities under the authority of the wartime ordinance, imprisoned 100 and ordered the others confined to their villages. During succeeding months, the police watched the ports of entry and directed all returning Sikhs to report to a central inquiry office at Ludhiana. There the police investigated each emigrant and jailed those they reckoned were ringleaders. The majority went free but were kept under surveillance.

Few arms found their way into India, and, with most of their leaders locked away, the *Ghadr*ites were an impotent force. A number did gather in gangs which wandered through several districts planning to plunder treasuries, raid arsenals, and attack police posts, but uncertain how to go about it. By early December 1914, the gangs had been broken up, or had dwindled away. The release of the *Komagata Maru* people seemed then to give the *Ghadr*ites a boost. A few passengers were recruited to the cause and their story was a spur to action. By January 1915, with the arrival of a Bengali master-revolutionary, Rashbehari Bose, the organizer behind the bomb thrown at Lord Hardinge in 1912, the *Ghadr*ites found the leadership they had been lacking. They carried out a number of violent robberies, made several attempts to derail trains, and set 21 February as the date for a rising.[21]

They counted on the 23rd Cavalry at Lahore to mutiny and to attack an arsenal at Mianmeer. This was to be the signal for simultaneous strikes at Ferozepore, Rawalpindi, and Meerut. During the second week of February, word went out to troops in cantonments throughout northern India. Bombs were prepared, and arms, such as the *Ghadr*ites had, collected. But scarcely a move was made without the knowledge of the police who had learned what was afoot from men arrested after a robbery in the Amritsar district. At the last moment, the police raided the *Ghadr* headquarters in Lahore on a signal from a spy they had planted in the heart of the conspiracy.[22]

There was no rising and the suspect troops were disarmed. The population gave the *Ghadr*ites no help, and in some cases actually chased them and turned them over to the police. Yet the Governor of the Panjab neither minimized the danger of the conspiracy nor saw fit to meet it with leniency. In March he summoned twelve leading members of the Sikh community to tell them they could avert bloodshed by co-operating with his government. There were by this time about 3,200 returned emigrants in the province, and local Sikh committees were quickly established to work with the police in dealing with them. At the same time, O'Dwyer obtained legislation permitting summary arrest and denying appeal against conviction. Beginning in April 1915, his government staged a series of conspiracy trials which, by the time the last judgment was handed down in May 1917, had involved 175 accused men and over 2,000 witnesses. Twenty men were hanged; seventy-six transported for life to the Andaman Islands, the convict colony for British India, and fifty-eight transported or imprisoned in India for shorter terms. Several hundred men were locked away without trial; many more were restricted to their villages; and the vernacular papers were vigorously suppressed.

Shortly after the conspiracy was broken, two *Komagata Maru* men were arrested: Gurmukh Singh outside one of the four houses used by the *Ghadr*ites in Lahore, and Bishen Singh in his village which he said he had not left.[23] They were convicted and Gurmukh Singh was transported for life. None of the *Komagata Maru* people were above suspicion, not even the fifty-nine who had boarded the train at Budge Budge and stayed out of trouble. Even these men were confined to their villages for the duration of the war, unable to find employment or to farm because they could not go to town for seed or other necessary business. Most of them leased their land and waited.[24]

The man who had carried revolvers from San Francisco to the *Komagata Maru* at Yokohama, Sohan Singh, was picked up by the police when he arrived at Calcutta. He was tried and sentenced to hang, although later spared by the Viceroy. By the autumn of 1915, four members of the Vancouver Shore Committee had fallen into the hands of the Indian police.[25] The most notable of them was Balwant Singh, the same Balwant who had met Gurdit

Singh in Moji in April 1914, and who had been arrested by American authorities at Sumas. Bela Singh, the eyes and ears of Hopkinson in Vancouver, and Dr Rughunath Singh told the court of a number of mutinous speeches that Balwant Singh had given—particularly his address to the passengers of the *Komagata Maru* at Moji and the one he gave at the first fund-raising for the *Komagata Maru* in Vancouver. Some witnesses accused him of advocating the murder of Malcolm Reid, Hopkinson, and Bela Singh. The court judged him a ringleader, and he was hanged in Lahore in 1917. It was a fate that Gurdit Singh had reason to fear.

II

SURRENDER

In March 1915, a number of Sikh pilgrims came to Hyderabad for the great spring festival, *Hola Mohalla*. They gathered at the shrine of Huzur Sahib at Nander where the tenth and last Guru, Gobind Singh, had died. Gurdit Singh made his way there, planning to steal back to the Panjab in their company. He travelled with them north by train for 800 kilometres before an instinct for safety told him to go no further. A year later, he was settled in Sipri, in the then Gwalior State, under the assumed name of Hari Singh. He had taken a contract for work on a reservoir and a canal, written to a friend for money, made a profit, and was weighing the purchase of a large acreage, when he was warned that the Panjab police knew where he was. He fled immediately, walking by night, as he had many times since Budge Budge, certain that the police were everywhere, that every interested stranger was a possible informant, that people he passed on the road were speaking his name, and driven by these fears to direct his steps across fields and jungle most of the way from Sipri to Bundi, about 240 kilometres to the west. Further wandering led him south and west through the famine-struck regions of Rajasthan to the then Baroda State in Gujarat which he reached in September 1916. He had some medical knowledge, and when he saw that he could utilize this profitably, he got some books, learned some more, and started a practice that brought in him a comfortable income.[1]

He had been living quietly in Baroda for a little over two and a half years when he learned of the Jallianwalla Bagh massacre. On 13 April 1919, during the religious and commercial festival of *Baisakhi*, the first day of the Hindu and Sikh New Year, a British general, Reginald Edward Harry Dyer, had broken up an assembly of many thousands of Sikh men, women, and children in Amritsar at Jallianwalla Bagh, an enclosed quadrangle of waste land. He had brought in a force of fifty Gurkha and Baluchi riflemen, opened fire without warning, continued until the last round was spent, and then marched his men off without regard for the wounded and dead he left behind. Strict censorship and martial law were immediately imposed on Amritsar and then extended to other districts, but word of what had happened came out nonetheless, and late in August the government finally admitted that 290 people had died. Many Indians believed that the number was much higher, yet the government was slow to investigate or to condemn General Dyer's action.

The wartime conspiracy trials had disturbed many Indians, but there had been some expectancy of greater independence when the war ended, which quickly turned to outrage when the government moved to buttress police powers—the purpose of the Rowlatt Act of March 1919. Gandhi, a new and untested force in Indian politics, launched a campaign of non-violent resistance with a national day of fasting, prayer, and strikes. Unfortunately riots and bloodshed had occurred. Then came the massacre at Amritsar, and for Gandhi the shocked conclusion that he had been deluded and that the British regime was wholly bad.[2]

Gurdit Singh followed these developments in the newspapers, in which he read Motilal Nehru's presidential address at the Amritsar Congress in December 1919. It was a Congress attended, in the wake of the terrible tragedy in that city, by 8,000 delegates from all parts of India, including all the leading figures in the nationalist struggle. In his three-hour address, as he surveyed the origins of the situation in the Panjab, Nehru briefly referred to the *Komagata Maru* incident which, he said, had marked a renewal of unrest and had been used by Sir Michael O'Dwyer as an excuse for extraordinary police measures. The speech was a balanced one, reflecting the preliminary findings of a special Congress sub-committee—on which both Motilal Nehru and Gandhi served—then conducting its own investigation parallel to the government's official Jallianwalla Bagh inquiry. When Nehru mentioned Budge Budge, he gave the facts without embroidery as he understood them: the passengers had been broken down by consistent ill-treatment and when they landed in India and found themselves prisoners 'they completely lost their heads and the unfortunate Budge Budge riot was the result'.[3]

This was close enough to the truth, but it was not what Gurdit
Singh wanted history to say. With this on his mind, he went to
Gandhi's ashram on the outskirts of Ahmedabad only to lose his
nerve when he met a Sikh he thought was a police agent. Not
long after this, he missed a chance to speak to B. G. Tilak who
came to Baroda but was surrounded by such a crush of people
that it was impossible to get near. He then decided to go to
Bombay which he knew would be visited from time to time by
all the nationalist leaders. The centre of town seemed too risky
so he took a job under the name Valdraja at a shipyard at Mahal
Bandar eighteen kilometres away. He was first hired as a doctor,
and then he took over as a manager. A friend gave him an intro-
duction to V. J. Patel, Congress leader of Gujarat, who received
him rather coldly, perhaps not believing in his identity, or perhaps
simply uninterested in his story. In early March 1920, Gandhi
came to Bombay to defend himself in a contempt of court case
arising from comments he had published in his paper *Young
India*. Gurdit Singh gained an audience but not in private, and,
with other people present, he was too fearful of the police to
say what he wanted to. Gandhi asked him his name.[4]

'I have no name; the one I have cannot be disclosed here; if
you still insist please allow me to speak with you privately for
fifteen minutes.'

'I have no time and there is no need for privacy.'

'Very important affairs I have to communicate—please allow
me at least five minutes.'

'I have absolutely no time at all.'

Several times Gurdit Singh returned to the house where Gandhi
was staying, but without getting the opening he was looking for.
Then in April the Panjab leader Pandit Rambhuj Dutt Chowdhari,
a man close to Gandhi, visited Bombay and on 19 April Gurdit
Singh managed to talk to him alone. He would not say who he
was, but got to the point quickly, attacking Motilal Nehru for
saying that the passengers at Budge Budge had lost their temper
and violated the law. 'The innocent passengers of the *Komagata
Maru* were the aggrieved party', he told Chowdhari: 'they remained calm up to the time of their death by a shower of bullets.'

Chowdhari observed that Nehru had merely repeated what the
official Inquiry Committee had reported. Gurdit Singh was ready
for this.

'You have most probably read the Government Report on Jallianwalla Bagh in which it is mentioned that only 290 people were dead. Is that true?'

Chowdhari said that it was absolutely false. The government had been suppressing the truth.

'Then now sir, how did you believe the Report of the Government Inquiry Committee?'

The comparison with Jallianwalla Bagh could not be shunted aside. 'Do you know the fact by guess or actual knowledge?' Chowdhari asked, and the charterer of the *Komagata Maru*, milking the moment for all it was worth, said that Gurdit Singh was still living and could tell the whole story.

'If he is alive can he come to me?' It was a testing question.

'Yes, Panditji, he is alive and whenever you will send for him he will come to you.'

'I want to see him today if possible, if not, as soon as he can.'

'If Gurdit Singh just now comes to you, how will you recognize him?'

'Yes, I shall be able to recognize him through my heart.'

'I am that unfortunate, always at your service.'

'Yes, you are one of the fortunate sufferers, but where is Gurdit Singh?'

'I am Gurdit Singh before you.'

Chowdhari embraced the old man. But rather than listen to the long tale he wanted to tell, Chowdhari asked him to write it down so it could be read later. It could wait. It was an old matter, and there was ammunition enough in the present.

Similarly, when Gurdit Singh sought out the great Panjab patriot, Lala Lajpat Rai, recently returned from exile in America, and Shanker Lal Banker, a Gandhi disciple and the organizer of the Ahmedabad mill-workers, neither man showed much interest in his case, and he must have begun to realize that he was not going to receive a warm welcome until he was among Sikhs. Late in the year he got a chance to speak to the Nehrus, Motilal and Jawaharlal, who came to Bombay to confer with other leaders about the Congress programme, and who were encouraging. Motilal was willing to admit a mistake and to do something about it at the Nagpur Congress in December, but Gurdit Singh fell ill and did not attend.[5]

At Nagpur the Congress abandoned its creed of constitutional

9

reform, and under Gandhi's sway adopted his programme of
non-violent non-cooperation which he promised would bring
independence within a year. The impetus came from the
Amritsar tragedy, which especially affected the Sikhs, but Sikh
agitation took a religious rather than a political form. Sikh purists
were demanding control of shrines which for generations had been
kept by priests of the *Sahajdhari* or slow adopters tradition: un-
bearded priests, indistinguishable from Hindus, priests who had
not been baptized into the militant order of the last Guru, Gobind
Singh, who served as a bridge between Hindu and Sikh, who
tolerated Hindu idols in Sikh shrines, and who enjoyed almost
proprietary rights over those shrines. The cause against these
priests had been maturing ever since the Singh Sabha movement—
encouraged by the British—had begun the work of de-Hinduizing
Sikhism in the latter part of the nineteenth century. It had turned
into a crusade in the aftermath of Jallianwalla Bagh when the
management of the Golden Temple at Amritsar, in a slavish display of loyalty, had presented a baptismal turban and sword to
General Dyer. In the name of the Sikh community, a Committee
of 175 announced in November 1920 that it was taking over all
the shrines. A corps of volunteers styling themselves the Akali
Dal, the army of immortals, sprang into existence to wrest the
shrines from their keepers. On 20 February 1921—one and a half
months after the Nagpur Congress—a band of 130 Akalis seeking
possession of the shrine at Nankana, the birthplace of Guru
Nanak, were ambushed by the shrine priest's 400-strong body-
guard and, soaked in paraffin, dragged dead and dying to a pile
of logs burning in a pit.[6]

Although the struggle over the shrines divided Hindu and Sikh
and even split the Sikh community, the atrocity at Nankana was
turned against the government. For Sikhs, it was Jallianwalla Bagh
all over again. They were told that the local authorities had been
aware that the priest was fortifying the shrine and laying in
munitions and yet had not acted. It was natural to suspect the
government of complicity, Gandhi said, and he appealed to Sikhs
to think of the tragedy in terms of Indian nationality and freedom
from British rule.[7]

When he read about Nankana in the vernacular press, Gurdit
Singh decided to return to the Panjab. He had lived for years in
fear of a summary arrest and internment that would silence him

and prevent him ever telling his story. Now he was drawn by the ferment in the Panjab and by a desire to take part as the hero of the *Komagata Maru*. He took leave of his employer, and, on 13 March, on the first leg of his journey, reached Ahmedabad. Through a friend, he at last managed to introduce himself to Gandhi, but he was not ready for Gandhi's uncompromising advice that he should give himself up, and, hungry for recognition, he carried on by way of Karachi, Sukkur, Montgomery, and Lahore, seeking out nationalist leaders at each stage.

He stayed for a while in Lahore, where he saw Chowdhari a second time, and then committed himself actively to Congress work, touring the Panjab incognito, supporting the non-cooperation campaign, speaking at Amritsar, Tarn Taran, Ludhiana, Ambala, Saharanpur, Hardwar, and Dehra Dun. That summer he met the principal Sikh nationalists and when the Central Sikh League gathered at Lyallpur at the end of the summer, several pamphlets were distributed announcing that Gurdit Singh would soon reveal himself. In September and October, Panjabi papers were regularly publishing a history of his adventures, and if he had been a forgotten figure a few months before, his name was now firmly established in the public mind.

On 4 and 5 November, as a delegate from Ambala, he attended the All-India Congress Committee meeting in Delhi, and he spoke to other delegates about surrendering to the police. The question of timing came up, and the December Congress session in Ahmedabad was suggested. Gandhi thought there should be no delay; it was not creditable to him that a patriot such as Gurdit Singh should be running from the police, but Gurdit Singh and his friends wished to make as much of the moment as they could, and they settled on the annual festival at Nankana held on 15 November, as explosive an occasion as they could choose.[8]

A week in advance, he advised the papers that he would appear at the festival and hand himself over to the authorities. On the morning of 15 November, he slipped into Nankana where 50,000 Sikhs had flocked, thousands of them wearing black turbans in honour of the Akalis murdered there nine months earlier. By prearrangement, following morning prayers, he stepped dramatically out of the crowd in the *gurdwara* and delivered a rousing speech. The police knew better than to provoke the Sikhs by going in after him, and he participated fully in the festival, addressing the assembly twice more that day, joining in the evening prayers, and watching the early-morning display of fireworks. Then on the afternoon of the second day, at a time set through an exchange of notes with the Police Commissioner, he led a vast procession to the Commissioner's bungalow, and as the pilgrims seated themselves in the field across the way—his son, his ancient father, and his elder sister among them—he walked up to the door and gave himself in. He had been a fugitive for seven years, one month, and seventeen days.

In the pages of *Young India*, Gandhi congratulated the Sikhs for remaining non-violent. 'It is no small matter', he wrote, 'for one to remain in hiding for seven years and escape the police and then openly to surrender oneself to them, yet Sardar Gurdit Singh has succeeded in performing the wonder.'⁹ His words were echoed by the Ahmedabad Congress which—meeting in the highly-charged atmosphere of the twelfth month of the non-cooperation campaign—found time to congratulate Gurdit Singh and the Sikhs who had kept the peace when he was arrested.

A sane government would not have bothered to prosecute, but that was not the outlook of the Panjab authorities. They were about to bundle Gurdit Singh onto a train for Calcutta to stand trial for his defiance of the police at Budge Budge, when they received word that the Bengal government did not want him. He could have been released at that moment; instead, he was sent to Dera Ghazi Khan in south-eastern Panjab where he was detained without trial until 28 February 1922. When he was released he made a grand return, speaking at every stop, arriving at Lahore on 4 March and Amritsar on 6 March. Thousands of people met him at the Amritsar station, and he addressed two rallies before the day was done. His language was inflammatory; he openly courted arrest. 'We sacrificed ourselves for the government', he said, referring to the Indian contribution in the World War, 'and what have we got in return?—Jallianwalla Bagh.' He claimed to be penniless; the government had taken ten thousand rupees in the name of the *Komagata Maru*, but he said, 'It does not matter if I have lost one lakh rupees; I will now pay the real price which is my life.'¹⁰

The next day, 7 March 1922, he was re-arrested, and on 12 March he was brought before a magistrate and charged with preaching sedition. He chose to defend himself—a departure from

Gandhian principles—to publicize his story and that of the *Komagata Maru*. His case was remanded several times, and the proceedings dragged on through April, May, and June. On 26 July, he was sentenced in Amritsar to imprisonment for five years. He was sixty-three years old.

He served the full five years at Mianwali prison in east Panjab (now Pakistan). The non-cooperation campaign had collapsed before he entered prison, although the attitude of the Panjab was still described as sullen. When he came out in 1927, the country was comparatively quiet. He took up residence in Calcutta where he carried on a futile suit—begun in prison—to gain reparation of 25,000 rupees for his *Komagata Maru* losses. His *Voyage of the Komagata Maru*, written before he was arrested at Nankana, was published privately in English about 1928. In 1929, he was elected as a delegate to the All-India Congress session in Lahore, and he continued to be an active Congress worker well into his seventies. During the renewed agitation of the early 1930's, he went to jail for five months in 1931, six in 1932, and a further period in 1933. *The Statesman*, an English-language daily in Calcutta, made the mistake of dredging up his past in an abusive article which linked him to the *Ghadr* conspiracy and the use of murder to achieve political ends. He won a libel suit against it in 1934–5 and was awarded Rs 2,000 compensation. In 1935, he ran for election to the Punjab Assembly as a Congress candidate in the Amritsar district, but his reputation as Babaji of *Komagata Maru* was not enough to carry a majority against a rising Sikh nationalist politician, Partap Singh Kairon, forty-one years his junior.

He complained that his encounters with the government had cost him all the money he had. 'I have to work very hard now at my age, seventy-nine years old', he wrote in July 1939 to Ramsharan Vidyarthi, who was undertaking his biography. 'I simply cannot get any time to write my own autobiography. The claim that I made against the British government for 20,000 rupees has been rejected. If the British government were a just government, then I would not have pressed for this claim. I have many many proofs that the government has given me a great deal of trouble and hardship for no crime. That is why I oppose the British government. The British government is very unjust to our countrymen and based on that I have made this the principle of my life that I am willing to uproot the government and establish independence for my country and it is for this I have suffered all kinds of hardships.'[11]

He had followed Gandhi's creed since 1920, and as a very old man he would not admit that he had ever adopted violent methods. The revolvers brought aboard at Yokohama were not mentioned in his account of the *Komagata Maru*. He avoided all reference to *Ghadr*ite activity among the passengers, and he insisted that they had been unarmed at Budge Budge and unable to strike out even in self-defence. He stuck to this story even after Indian independence which he lived to see. In September 1947 when he presided over a public meeting in Calcutta on the thirty-second anniversary of the death of the Bengal revolutionary, Jatindranath Mukerjee, he said that the *Komagata Maru* had been a commercial venture, not a political one. He wanted to reveal the innocence of the men who were denied entry to Canada and fired on by police and troops in India.[12]

The *Komagata Maru* preoccupied him to the end. In September 1951 he wrote to the Prime Minister, Nehru, to say he was not keeping well and that it was his wish to see a memorial to the passengers erected while he was still alive. The Bengal government was involved in the project and Gurdit Singh helped to choose the site. Nehru unveiled the completed monument on 1 January 1952. In the autumn of 1953, Gurdit Singh began to weaken and in January 1954 his friends brought him back to Amritsar from Calcutta for a change. He expressed a desire to see the passengers of the *Komagata Maru* before he died, and the Punjab Sikh Youth Federation of Amritsar organized a *Kavi Darbar*, a poetry festival, to commemorate the martyrs of the *Komagata Maru*. It was held on 4 July 1954 and Gurdit Singh presided. He died twenty days later at the end of his ninety-fifth year.

12

ASSASSINATION

A couple of weeks after the *Komagata Maru* was chased out of Vancouver, Hopkinson went down to Portland and Astoria to see informants there, particularly a Muslim named Mahommed Din, a double-dealing leader among the Indians in Oregon. From the latter he learned that a number of Sikhs were leaving for San Francisco to join a contingent sailing for India in a few days. All this was being organized by Bhagwan Singh Jakh and Maulvi Barkatullah, late of Tokyo, leaders of the *Ghadr* party since Har Dayal had left for Switzerland under threat of deportation. On the day that Britain went to war, they had called for volunteers for the mutiny whose time had come. At Fresno, at Sacramento, at Portland, and at Astoria they were recruiting men and money, planning to send 200 or 300 Sikhs at once and more to follow, promising that arms would be ready for them on arrival. All the native troops in India would rise at once, they said, and the Ameer of Afganistan was standing by with arms and ammunition for 1,000,000 men.[1] As it turned out, the men who went back first, found Commissioner Halliday standing by with a passport for jail.

Hopkinson warned the British Consul-General in San Francisco and asked him to watch departures there. In Canada, as well, the revolutionary party was arranging a general return to India, and Malcolm Reid, put wise by Hopkinson, was now as anxious to stop men going out as he had been to keep the *Komagata Maru* people from coming in.

Bela Singh, Hopkinson's chief tipster, on the government payroll for $62.50 a month, was sent down to the docks at Vancouver and Victoria to scrutinize the Sikhs sailing on the 22nd and 25th of August. His pocket bulged; with a revolver, he told the men he interviewed to intimidate them. Forty-five boarded nonetheless, but Bela Singh had their names, and Hopkinson was able to send the Indian authorities word on who was seditious and who was not.[2]

On the last day of the month, a Vancouver man, walking the railway track through the Kitsilano Indian reserve a few kilometres west of the main downtown area, came across a decomposed body in the grass and bushes. It was a Sikh, Harnam Singh, a friend of Bela Singh, a man who had also worked for the immigration department. There was an empty whiskey flask nearby. His turban was tied around his feet and his throat had been slashed from ear to ear.[3]

Three days later, in a boarding house on Third Avenue, another of Bela Singh's set, Arjan Singh by name, was shot in the throat —whether by accident, as eleven men testified, or by design. Ever since Bela Singh had first gone to Immigration—in the Bhagwan Singh case—Rahim and the revolutionaries who ran the *gurdwara* had been demanding his life and those of his closest friends, Baboo Singh and Ganga Ram. But Bela Singh was himself a rough-and-ready fighting man, a bold bully who used his influence with Immigration to frighten his countrymen and to extract his due from them. On 30 September he had entered the lion's den, accepting an invitation from the revolutionary party to meet in the *gurdwara*—a place he had been avoiding—to settle differences. A number of his followers had gathered outside, clutching sticks. His friend, Baboo Singh, fearing foul play, had sent for the police, and his enemies, if they had any plans, chose not to carry them out.[4]

He came back on the evening of the 5th for Arjan Singh's funeral, climbing the stairs to the *gurdwara*, which was on the second floor, and entering by the rear door. There were thirty-eight people there including the priests, Bhag Singh and Balwant Singh, and Sohan Lal, a small, quick man who throughout the summer had been the chief link between the Shore Committee and the attorney Bird. Some time after Bela Singh sat himself on the floor near the front, there were shots, a flurry of them. Journalist Bruce McKelvie who lived nearby was on his way to catch a streetcar a few minutes after 7 when he heard a single shot and then after a brief interval a fusillade, followed by another interval and one last shot.[5] The police, arriving minutes later, found three Sikhs wounded on the floor, one near the rear door, shot through the left side from behind, another braced against the west wall, shot in the knee, and about one metre from him, the priest Bhag Singh with bullets through the lungs and abdomen. A trail of blood led from the *gurdwara* steps to the building next door where several more men had fled for shelter, some of them leaping from a second-storey porch in their haste to get away. One of them, Badan Singh, a resident of the *gurdwara*, had been shot four times in the upper part of his body.

Bela Singh was arrested in the street, standing by an ambulance watching as the wounded, nine in number, were carted off. One of the revolvers used in the shooting was found in front of the *gurdwara;* another in Bela Singh's house along with nearly 300 cartridges and other ammunition. In the operating room of the General Hospital, as the doctors swabbed and stitched, a justice of the peace, Hopkinson, and the police, with Bela Singh in tow, took depositions. 'I am going to die. You can do nothing to help me', Bhag Singh said before he gave his statement, and while it was being read back, he breathed his last.[6] Badan Singh also died shortly after he was admitted.

Bhag Singh and most of the injured men told the same story. They said that Bela Singh, having entered, thrown his coin into the collection pot, and taken a place on the floor near the front, had leapt to his feet while they were at prayer and had fired at Bhag Singh with two revolvers. And when there was a general rush to escape, he had turned his weapons on the rest.

But there were other witnesses, friends of Bela Singh, who said that he had fired in self-defence. He sat close to Bhag Singh, a little to one side, and they had argued during the service. Just as the singing and prayers finished, Badan Singh had come across the room saying, 'I fix him myself,' pulling a black pistol from his pocket. Bela Singh ran to the back; Badan Singh fired, and Bhag Singh reached for the holy sword under the altar. Then there were a lot of shots and a confused scramble for the exits.[6]

The coroner held his inquest on Wednesday, 9 September, and Bela Singh was subsequently committed for trial. For the defence, it was essential to show that there had been earlier threats against him, and while his friends would testify and Dr Rughunath Singh, still in Vancouver, would take the stand, Inspector Hopkinson's testimony was especially wanted. The immigration department had statements dating back to December 1913, taken from men who had heard Rahim, Sohan Lal, and members of the *gurdwara* committee talk of murdering not only Bela Singh, Baboo Singh, and Ganga Ram, but Hopkinson and Malcolm Reid as well.[7] Hopkinson could testify to this.

When the criminal assizes began in mid-October, Bela Singh's case was not brought forward right away, but all the witnesses were required to report each morning and to hold themselves in readiness. On the 21st of October, as he waited in a corridor of the provincial courthouse in Vancouver, Hopkinson was shot down by Mewa Singh, a man well-known to him, one of the four arrested in July carrying revolvers purchased in the United States. Hopkinson was standing outside the witness room, hands in pockets, when Mewa Singh stepped up to him, drawing a nickel-plated .32 calibre revolver and firing from point-blank range. The inspector sank to his knees, grabbing Mewa Singh around the thigh. Mewa Singh, short and fleshy, clubbed him over the head with the revolver held in his right hand and then, dropping it and transferring a snub-nosed revolver from his left to his right, went on firing, jumping in the air and throwing up his arm each time he pulled the trigger.[8]

Several men in the witness room saw the shooting, but trans-fixed or frightened, did not move except to close the door. Richard Polley, an employee of the court, only a few metres away when all the shots were fired, walked up to Mewa Singh and demanded the guns, but he replied, 'I give them to the police.' James McCann, head janitor, charged upstairs after the first shot, rushed the Sikh, overpowered him, and wrested the weapons from him. 'I shoot', Mewa Singh said, 'I go to station.' By the time the doctors arrived, and there were two in the building, Hopkinson was dead.

Civic and federal officials organized one of the greatest funeral processions the city had ever seen. More than 2,000 marched—militia, police, and firemen, immigration and customs officials, men from the United States immigration service, C.P.R. employees, and a strong contingent from the Orange Lodge to which Hop-kinson had belonged. Every Indian along the route was covered by a plainclothesman, the police taking no chances with reports that Malcolm Reid and their own chief were targets.[9]

Lewis Harcourt, the British Colonial Secretary, had praised Hopkinson's work in connection with the *Komagata Maru*—as had the Secretary of State for India—and he asked immediately how Hopkinson's family was fixed. There was a widow, Nellie, a girl from London's Highgate district trained as a stenographer; and there were daughters, Jean and Constance, aged six and two, both born in Vancouver. As it turned out, Nellie Hopkinson could not get an Indian civil service pension because her husband had been employed only indirectly by the Indian government. A lump sum payment was promised, but that was a matter of negotiation between governments and was not produced without delay, if it was produced at all. The Canadian immigration department did what it could for her, offering her a job as a stenographer in the Vancouver office, and she worked there from February 1915 until 1921 when she moved to California to join her family there.[10]

The India Office decided against replacing Hopkinson. That did not mean that the work he had been doing was abandoned, but, for one reason or another, it seemed best not to entrust it to an officer in the employment of the Canadian immigration branch. It was a decision that the Canadian government readily accepted, happy to leave to the Indian authorities their own intelligence gathering. 'I am afraid', said Superintendent Scott, 'that Inspector Hopkinson lost his life largely through the fact that he was performing services of a dual character and that one set of duties rather jeopardized his position in regard to the other.'[11]

Malcolm Reid was removed to Ottawa for a month for his own safety, and E. Blake Robertson, the Deputy Superintendent of Immigration, came to Vancouver to take charge in his place. Robertson looked around, talked to the staff, and decided that Reid should not come back, that he was incompetent. He tried to push him into the police force, but Reid would not go. Robertson recommended Lethbridge, Alberta at the same rank and rate of pay but Reid wanted to stay in Vancouver and in the end he was allowed to do so as Dominion Immigration Inspector for British Columbia without any authority over Vancouver or Victoria, the two ports that really counted. Tucked away in an upstairs office in the Vancouver immigration building, he remained for years a nuisance to a succession of immigration agents.[12]

None of the officials thought that Mewa Singh had acted on his own. As they knew him, he was too pliant and fearful. Malcolm Reid said right after the shooting that Mewa Singh was the last man he would have suspected.[13]

Hopkinson had seen a lot of him, especially after 17 July when, in the midst of the *Komagata Maru* excitement, he had been arrested coming through the woods along the American border carrying 500 rounds of ammunition and a revolver. He had gone shopping with the now-dead Bhag Singh, and with Balwant Singh and Harnam Singh of Sahri, another leading figure in the British Columbia Sikh population. They had met Taraknath Das in Sumas on the American side of the border and had gone into two hardware stores to buy several .32 calibre automatics and boxes of shells. A few pistols would have served revolutionary propaganda well if, put into the hands of the *Komagata Maru* passengers, they had been used to provoke police retaliation.[14] But Mewa Singh, sent back first, had fallen into the hands of the Canadian authorities, and the Americans, alerted, had stopped the others, although they released Bhag Singh and Balwant Singh without charges after two weeks. Harnam Singh, less fortunate, had been ordered deported to India because the Canadians were able to show that he had no legal residence in Canada. (He had already been deported from Canada once.)

Things will go better for you, Mewa Singh had been warned, if you tell us what your friends have been up to. He could have been charged with carrying a concealed weapon and fined $50, or he could have been locked away for ten years for evading customs with a pistol in his possession. That had been his choice. His trial had been adjourned once so that he could think it over, and when he had finally given a statement against his friends, he had been let off with the lesser charge.[15]

His story had not satisfied the officials, but he had told them he was frightened for his life, and Hopkinson had borne with him, hoping to get more out of him later. In August and September, Hopkinson had worked on him, 'befriended' him, and the immigration inspector could not have been more surprised when Mewa Singh came at him with a gun.

Blake Robertson judged him a weak-minded man who had betrayed his own countrymen, and, when they put pressure on him, had shot Hopkinson to atone. But the Sikhs were told by their people that Mewa Singh had endeared himself to Hopkinson and had acted as his informer so that he could get a chance to take revenge. He was, they said, a true hero and martyr.[16]

Ten days after the shooting, Mewa Singh was tried for murder
and sentenced to hang. Bela Singh's trial had been pushed back
so that the state could bring down a swift and certain verdict.
There was no defence. A crowded courtroom, filled with whites
—all but four Sikhs stopped at the door—heard evidence, verdict,
and sentence all within an hour and forty minutes. Mewa Singh,
repeatedly wiping his eyes, wanted to plead guilty; his lawyer
waived all cross-examination, and the crown attorney cut his case
short. 'I know I have shot Mr Hopkinson and I will have to die',
Mewa Singh declared in an eleven-page rambling statement that
his lawyer read out for him. He blamed Hopkinson and Reid for
the desecration of the *gurdwara* at the hands of Bela Singh, 'You,
as Christians, would you think there was any more good left in
your church if you saw people shot down and killed in it . . . ?' He
said he was a God-fearing man who prayed for an hour in the
morning and an hour-and-a-half at night and he could not turn
his back when wrong was done. Hopkinson had tried to force
him to give evidence in favour of Bela Singh, and he had killed
the inspector to uphold the principles and honour of his religion.[17]

He wanted Bhag Singh's little daughter brought into the courtroom to hear him. Bhag Singh's wife, Harnam Kor, had died the
previous spring, still in her twenties. Their orphaned daughter,
now nearly three, was the infant born in Hong Kong on the way
to Canada and ordered deported with her mother on arrival in
Vancouver in January 1912. When she could not be found in
the crowd outside the courtroom, Mewa Singh broke into a
chant, startling and discomfiting almost everyone present. The
words, explained the court interpreter, an English woman, came
from the Sikh scriptures. They said it was the duty of a good
man to give his life for a good cause. And Mewa Singh wanted
everyone to know that the condition of the Hindus in Vancouver
was as bad as when the Muslims ruled India.

He gave no sign of distress when sentence was passed and
walked steadily, head bowed, back to his cell.

Within the week, Bela Singh was brought to trial. Bhag Singh's
dying deposition was read, as was a statement that had been prepared by Hopkinson. Sohan Lal, nursing a bullet wound in the
right knee, and a string of Sikhs from the *gurdwara* told one
story, while the friends of Bela Singh told another. The judge,

in charging the jury, left little doubt that he thought the prisoner should be acquitted, but the jury went out for four hours and failed to reach a verdict.

Two weeks later, after a second trial before the same judge and a new jury, Bela Singh was set free.[18]

Husain Rahim, Balwant Singh, Sohan Lal, Mitt Singh, and Kartar Singh, all members of the Shore Committee, were arrested on the charge of procuring Mewa Singh to murder Hopkinson. Sohan Lal, brought to trial first, was acquitted in the face of wildly conflicting testimony, and the authorities abandoned prosecution of the others.[19]

Balwant Singh with Kartar Singh left in late December 1914, staying a few days at *Ghadr* headquarters in San Francisco and spending several months in Shanghai, apparently preaching the *Ghadr* message. In July 1915 he turned up in Bangkok, and after British agents laid information against him, was deported to Singapore by the Siamese government. From Singapore he was shipped to the Panjab for trial at Lahore. Witnesses from Canada told the court that he had been a suspect in Hopkinson's murder and that helped to hang him. Kartar Singh who went to India ahead of Balwant Singh, only to be taken into custody within a few days of arrival, was also sentenced to death. In his case, the penalty was later reduced to life imprisonment.[20]

The informer, Bela Singh, walked unscathed through the streets of Vancouver, though he was a dangerous man to be around. On 18 March 1915, he escaped with a bullet through the coat when two of his companions were shot at—one killed—after running into Jagat Singh, a *Ghadr* supporter, in a Sikh store on Granville Street. In April, a dynamite explosion blew off the entire front end of a Third Avenue frame boarding house in which a number of Bela Singh's friends were asleep.[21] Three days later, Bela Singh was arrested for assault when the police arrived on the scene and saw him pummelling one of his opponents. He was sentenced to twelve months and served his time at the Burnaby prison farm along with Baboo Singh who had been convicted of forgery. Even then he kept feeding information to Reid, expecting to get out. But Reid no longer had much influence, and a Special Commissioner investigating the Indian situation said that jail was the best place for Bela Singh, that he should have been hanged, and that, if he wasn't kept in jail, he should be deported because he was a menace to the peace of the community.[22]

When he was released in 1916, he returned to India and in Hoshiarpur, in August 1916, he was questioned by Inspector Ikram-ul-Haq who got his name from Rughunath Singh. He gave the inspector the names of several more men of the 'loyal' party, and it was his testimony and theirs which sent Balwant Singh to the gallows.

In 1922–3, when terrorists—many of them old *Ghadr*ites—struck repeatedly in Jullunder and Hoshiarpur, the police turned again to Bela Singh. Ten years later, on a June evening, on the road back from Hoshiarpur, he was trapped outside his village of Jaina by some of these men and chopped to pieces.[23]

Husain Rahim, preferring the safety of exile, stayed in Vancouver until the end of the war, although he got nothing out of Martin Burrell's promise of sympathetic consideration for *Komagata Maru* claims. H. C. Clogstoun of Duncan, British Columbia, a retired Indian Civil Service officer, had been appointed to look into the matter, and predictably he had recommended no compensation. Instead he had suggested that the government give legal aid to anyone going to court to recover contributions to the *Komagata Maru* fund. The idea was to drive a wedge between the revolutionaries and the rest of the Indian community. In time, a handful of men brought a suit against Rahim and the estate of Bhag Singh, and they won judgments totalling a little over $2,000. Of course, as everyone knew, the money Rahim had controlled was long gone, some to Gurdit Singh, the rest for *Ghadr* projects in India, and Rahim, who had closed his supply and trust company and moved into a couple of short-lived lumber dealerships, had no assets to be attached. So to clear the air the government paid the claims of those who had gone to court, satisfied that the seditionists had been discredited.[24]

While on the surface all was much quieter in Vancouver after 1915, the sense of being embattled which Canadian Indians felt was not gone. They still accepted the leadership of men like Mitt Singh, Mohammed Akbar, and Gurdit Singh of Bilga (another Gurdit Singh), men who had been active in the *Komagata Maru* affair and who remained sympathetic to the *Ghadr* cause. Mewa Singh, venerated in *Ghadr* party literature, was remembered on the anniversary of his execution on 11 January 1915. In 1917, Sikhs gathered for three days at the *gurdwara* at Fraser Mills where he had been cremated. Five hundred came the next year when there were scarcely 1,000 Sikhs in the province, and in succeeding years right to the present, the occasion has been marked in *gurdwaras* both in Canada and the United States.[25]

From the beginning the *Ghadr* party had looked to Germany for help, and with the outbreak of war, German money and expertise were there for the asking, although the problem of delivering them to India was never solved. When the United States entered the war in 1917, the American government succumbed to British diplomatic pressure and indicted 105 men—Indians, Germans, and Americans—on the charge of violating American neutrality. Thirty-five were brought to trial in a conspiracy case staged in San Francisco at a cost to the American government of an estimated $450,000.[26] Bhagwan Singh Jakh was sentenced to eighteen months, served at San Quentin, and Taraknath Das got twenty-two months. Both men settled in the United States after their release, Bhagwan Singh returning to India only in 1958. The *Ghadr* party itself survived the ordeal, and shifting from alignment with Germany to Soviet Russia, remained active on the Pacific coast until 1947 when it was disbanded with the achievement of Indian independence.[27]

When the first World War ended, there were 900 or 1,000 Indians left in British Columbia—nearly 1,000 having gone in 1914–15. The exodus might well have been greater, but by the summer of 1915, it was known that returning emigrants were being arrested wholesale by the Indian police. A bloody vendetta and the murder of a government officer had done nothing to erase prejudice in British Columbia, and few Canadians would have objected if the government had stuck to a rigid exclusionist policy which would have meant, in time, the complete disappearance of the Indian community. However, at the Imperial War Conference of 1918, Prime Minister Borden agreed to admit the wives and minor children of men already in the country. He bent to the pressure of British officials who told him that the stakes were high, that the atmosphere in the Panjab, the chief recruiting ground for the Indian army, was being poisoned by agitators making skilful use of the Canadian situation; and he recognized the damage done by the *Komagata Maru*.[28]

A few men did bring in wives and children after 1918, but not many, apparently because most could not afford it. No other

immigration was allowed, so that over the next decade and more
the population neither grew nor changed much, remaining essen-
tially the same group that had come into the country in 1904–8
and stayed throughout the war. These people continued to find
work in the saw mills and shingle mills of the lower Fraser valley
and Vancouver Island, or the lumber camps of the interior.
During the depression some turned to small businesses, importing
tea or, in the Vancouver and Victoria areas, delivering firewood
and coal; and there were among them two notable entrepreneurs,
Kapur Singh and Mayo Singh, owners of the Kapoor Mill at
Barnet and the Mayo Mill at Duncan. But forty years after the
first had immigrated, none enjoyed the rights of Canadian citizenship. The franchise disqualifications under British Columbian provincial law stayed in force up to 1947–8; and there were other
disabilities—exclusion from mechanical unions, from employment
in public and municipal works, and from the professions of law
and pharmacy, the last affecting the prospects of Canadian-born
Sikhs pushed through high school by their parents.

By 1941, there were no more than 1,500 Indians in Canada, a
largely male population, with a preponderance in the age-range
fifty to sixty-five. Over the years, about 180 women had been
brought in—most of them much younger than their husbands—
and their Canadian-born children, some reaching adulthood, numbered 424. There had, of course, been illegal immigration: students
overstaying their visas, American Sikhs slipping over the border,
and youths misrepresenting themselves as the children of Canadian residents. The authorities took action when they could, but
depended on information from within the community and that
information generally surfaced for the worst of motives. In 1939,
the Khalsa Diwan found a champion in Dr D. P. Pandia, a man
who had been Gandhi's secretary for a brief time and who visited
Vancouver on a lecture tour. With the outbreak of war, the
Department of External Affairs, remembering the *Komagata
Maru*, was anxious to avoid offending the public in India.[29] Pandia
played this for what it was worth, and, as a consequence, over
200 illegal immigrants were registered and given resident status.

Throughout the war, Pandia agitated both in Canada and in
the United States for enfranchisement and changes in immigration
law. In 1945, a Co-operative Commonwealth Federation motion
to grant the franchise was defeated in the British Columbian legis-

10

lature by two votes. The Canadian government had never been courageous about tackling prejudice, but the postwar situation called for some action. The Indian National Congress had actively supported the claims of Indians overseas, especially in the British Dominions; and, as India moved towards independence, the position of the Indian minority in Canada became a greater embarrassment. The human rights provisions of the United Nations Charter and the liberalization of American law pushed Canada along. In an expanding economy with a booming lumber industry, opposition to immigration from Asia was muted. But nothing would have been accomplished without a well-organized, low-profile, effort by the Indian community on its own behalf.[30] Following Indian independence in 1947, the British Columbian legislature finally extended the franchise, and with that full citizenship was given to resident Indians in the province. It all went to prove Rahim and his friends right when they said that Indians could expect no justice overseas until they enjoyed self-rule at home.

In the 1950's the Khalsa Diwan campaigned quietly for the extension of immigrant categories to include family members besides spouse or minor child, but though they had the support of a few members of parliament, changes came slowly. In 1951, Canada agreed to admit a small number of Indian immigrants besides those with a sponsoring parent or spouse. The quota, first set at 150, 100, and 50 for India, Pakistan, and Sri Lanka respectively and in 1958 increased to 300 for India, was filled by technically skilled or professionally qualified people. In 1962 when Ellen Fairclough, the Minister for Citizenship and Immigration, proudly announced new non-discriminatory regulations, she also made it clear, contrary as it sounded, that there would be quotas for India, Pakistan, and Sri Lanka. From 1962 to 1967, immigration from India averaged 2,500 a year, a large intake compared with the past, but still not a great part of the total immigration to Canada.

With the changes in immigration regulations introduced by the Liberal government in 1967, the numbers have risen dramatically. Immigrants have come from new areas, the Deccan, Gujarat, Fiji, and East Africa, as well as the Panjab; and the old Sikh families with roots in Canada going back to the beginning of the century now make up a small element of the whole Indian population. But the *Komagata Maru* has not been forgotten, and Mewa Singh's picture still hangs prominently in the Vancouver Sikh temple.

Notes

Chapter 1: EXCLUSION

1   Hopkinson is listed in *Thackers Directory*, 1907, as Inspector of Police, section B, 18 Cossipore Rd., Calcutta. He appears in the *Vancouver Directory* for the first time in 1908 at 551 Richards. At the time of his death, there was some confusion about his place and date of birth. The baptismal records of the India Office Library show Delhi, 16 June 1880.

2   In 1913–14, Hopkinson was paid £60 a year plus £60 expenses by the India Office. For work in connection with the US immigration office in Vancouver, he was paid $25 a month. At that time, he received $125 a month from the Canadian government: Immigration 808722(1), Record Group 76, Public Archives Canada; also Auditor General's Report, 1913–14.

3   All sums mentioned are in 1914 yen, dollars or rupees.

4   D. S. Dady Burjor, a Parsee cigar importer and part-time interpreter for American immigration authorities in San Francisco, described savings on this scale in a report to Hopkinson, 30 Jan. 1914: C.O. [Colonial Office] 42/978, microfilm, Public Archives Canada. So does a Canadian correspondent to *The Pioneer Mail*, Allahabad, 25 June 1914. One Sikh, arriving on the *Tosa Maru* at Calcutta after some years in North America, had reportedly accumulated $11,000: *Pioneer Mail*, 6 Nov. 1914.

5   The point is made by T. R. E. McInnes in his confidential report to Frank Oliver, Minister of the Interior, 2 Oct. 1907: copy, Borden Papers, Public Archives Canada. Often repeated is the story that Sikhs were attracted to Canada after a Sikh regiment had crossed the country by train following Queen Victoria's Jubilee in 1897. This was first offered as a reason for Sikh immigration by David E. Brown, General Superintendent of the Trans-Pacific Service of the C.P.R., when he appeared before Mackenzie King's Oriental Immigration Commission in Nov. 1907. King thought it unlikely and put the responsibility on the steamship companies which meant, in particular, the C.P.R.

6   *The Vancouver Daily Province*, 20 Oct. 1906.

7   E. Blake Robertson, Assistant Superintendent, to W. D. Scott, Superintendent of Immigration, 27 Dec. 1906, and Col. Falkland Warren to Under-Secretary of State for India, copy, 2 Jan. 1907, Immigration 536999(1).

8   McInnes to Oliver, 2 Oct. 1907.

9   Telegram from Viceroy enclosed in Elgin to Grey, 12 Feb. 1908, copy,

Immigration 536999(2); Mackenzie King to Laurier, 31 Jan. 1909, Laurier Papers, Public Archives Canada. Subsequent correspondence from India affirmed the same position. The Canadian government tried to stop the Indian influx with a continuous passage order-in-council issued 8 Jan. 1908, but it was loosely drafted and successfully challenged in court: *British Columbia Reports*, XIII, pp. 415–16. A new continuous passage order, underpinned by an amendment to the Immigration Act, was issued on 27 May 1908, and this was followed by a $200 requirement order on 3 June. These orders were directed against Indians and not the Chinese or Japanese who were covered by other legislation or by treaty. This is clearly stated in a memo from the Minister of the Interior of approximately 5 May 1908: Immigration 536999(3). After the passage of a new Immigration Act in 1910, these orders were reissued unchanged as P.C. 920 and P.C. 926.

10 The dubious legal basis of US Immigration Bureau practice was admitted in an internal memo on Hindu migration filed by the Bureau, 22 Jan. 1914: U. S. Immigration 52903/110, Record Group 85, National Archives, Washington.

11 Teja Singh to J. H. Hill [J. H. MacGill], Vancouver Immigration Agent, 24 Dec. 1908, and MacGill to W. W. Cory, Deputy Minister of the Interior, 21 Jan. and 12 Feb. 1909, Immigration 536999(3). A full account of the Honduras story is given in J. B. Harkin, *The East Indians in British Columbia* (Dept. of the Interior, 1909).

12 Extract from *Liverpool Courier*, 21 May 1908, Immigration 536999(2); Col. E. J. E. Swayne, Governor of British Honduras, confidential memorandum on the Indian community in British Columbia, Dec. 1908, Asiatic Immigration (Confidential Prints), Borden Papers. Police reports on Taraknath were compiled by the Criminal Intelligence Dept. in Delhi along with a host of similar records. During the first World War, a confidential summary was prepared by James Campbell Ker, formerly personal assistant to the Director of Criminal Intelligence. This document, covering the period 1907–17 and titled *Political Trouble in India*, was prepared for senior officials in the British Indian government to give them an overview that weekly intelligence reports, read and burned, never could do. In 1973 *Political Trouble in India* was reprinted and published by Oriental Publishers, Delhi, and it is an invaluable source. Taraknath's background is given on pp. 119–20.

13 Hopkinson, in an affidavit sworn 7 Dec. 1908, and reproduced in Harkin, *The East Indians in British Columbia*, said he was 'formerly of the City of Calcutta; for 4 years an Inspector of the Metropolitan Police.' Governor Swayne, who had come to British Columbia to recruit Indian labourers for British Honduras and had picked up a lot of information from Hopkinson, reported in Dec. 1908 that Hopkinson was on leave from the Calcutta police force. He also recommended that Hopkinson be appointed a Dominion Police officer in communication with the head of the Calcutta police.

14 Ker, *Political Trouble in India*, pp. 230–1.

15 Petition of 130 Indians from Vancouver and Victoria, 20–9 July 1910, MacGill to Scott, 15 July 1910, G. D. Kummar to L. M. Fortier, Superintendent of Immigration, 25 Aug. 1911, Immigration 808722(1); MacGill to Scott, 25 Oct. 1911, Immigration 808722(4).

16 MacGill to Cory, 28 Oct. 1910, Asiatic Immigration, Borden Papers. Rahim later claimed at a public meeting that all he was carrying was a cutting from the *World* which gave a history of explosives: Hopkinson's report of a meeting at O'Brien Hall, Vancouver, 29 Sept. 1913, US Immigration 52903/110. However, MacGill, reporting the day after Rahim's arrest, referred to a bomb-making process written into Rahim's notebook in a hand that was hard to decipher.

17 Harry Gwyther to Immigration Agent, Vancouver, 24 Feb. 1913, Immigration 536999(5).

18 April 1911 issue. Extract given in Ker, p. 201.

19 Ker, p. 128.

20 Emily C. Brown, *Har Dayal : Hindu Revolutionary and Rationalist* (Tucson: Arizona University Press, 1975), pp. 131–2.

21 Gwyther to Immigration Agent, 24 Feb. 1913.

22 Hopkinson to Cory, 11 June 1912, Immigration 536999(5).

23 Swayne, confidential memorandum, Dec. 1908; Brij Lal, 'East Indians in British Columbia, 1904–14: An Historical Study in Growth and Interpretation', M. A. Thesis, University of British Columbia, 1976, p. 69; Arun Coomer Bose, *Indian Revolutionaries Abroad* (Patna: Bharati Biwan, 1971), p. 52.

24 MacGill to Scott, letters one and two, 22 Jan. 1912; Scott to Cory, 1 April 1912, Immigration 536999(4); Malcolm Reid to Cory, 4 June 1912, Immigration 536999(5); [F. C. Blair] Private memorandum re Hindu immigration, particularly with reference to admission of wives and families, copy, H. H. Stevens Papers, City Archives, Vancouver; E. D. McLaren and Geo. C. Pidgeon, 'East Indian Immigration', *Westminster Hall Magazine*, Jan. 1912.

25 Memo on individual cases re Indian immigration to Canada, Immigration 536999(4); Memorandum of conversation with Sundar Singh, 29 May 1914, Loring Christie Papers, Public Archives, Canada; Hopkinson to Cory, 11 Jan. 1911, Immigration 536999(3).

26 Brown, p. 84, quoting from an article by Har Dayal, 'India in America', *The Modern Review*, July 1911, pp. 1–11.

27 Hopkinson's report of meeting at O'Brien Hall, 29 Sept. 1913.

Chapter 2: ENCOURAGEMENT

1 The discipline of the *Ghadr* party was explained by a witness in the 1917–18 San Francisco trial of *Ghadr* leaders: The United States of America vs. Franz Bopp *et al*, XII, p. 1053. This testimony is quoted by Emily C. Brown, p. 143.

2 Ker, *Political Trouble in India*, p. 128.

3	Immigration Inspector, Astoria, Oregon, to Immigration Inspector, Portland, 14 Jan. 1914, copy, C.O. 42/978.

4	Bose, *Indian Revolutionaries Abroad*, pp. 262–3; Minutes of a Board of Inquiry into the matter of Natha Singh, alias Bhagwan Singh, 21 Oct. 1913, copy, Stevens Papers.

5	Lahore Conspiracy Case Judgment, 13 Sept. 1915, Pt. III, A(1) The beginnings of conspiracy and war, p. 4, National Archives of India.

6	Hopkinson to Cory, 25 Oct. 1913, Immigration 536999(6). Lost domicile is discussed in Fortier to Cory, 17 June 1912, Immigration 536999(5).

7	Minutes of a Board of Inquiry into the matter of Gurdit Singh, son of Partab Singh, 22 Oct. 1913, Immigration 536999(7).

8	Hopkinson to Cory, 20 Oct 1913, Immigration 536999(6).

9	Malcolm Reid to Stevens, 30 April 1913, Stevens Papers. Stevens' hand in firing J. H. MacGill, a Liberal appointee, to bring in Reid is evident in the correspondence in MacGill's file: Immigration 334241. In an interview on 29 Oct. 1976, Fred 'Cyclone' Taylor, who had been one of Reid's immigration inspectors, said yes, Stevens got Reid the job after his predecessor was booted out.

10	T. R. E. McInnes to Robert Borden, 2 Dec. 1913, Borden Papers.

11	Hunter had been threatened with impeachment, but in the end was simply admonished by Laurier who had appointed him. The British Columbian government reduced the importance of the Chief Justiceship by creating a Court of Appeal superior to the Supreme Court that Hunter headed: Laurier to Dunsmuir, 10 Feb. 1909, and Laurier to Hunter, 6 April 1909, Laurier Papers.

12	*Daily Province*, 1 Dec. 1913.

13	*The Sun*, Vancouver, 15 Dec. 1913.

14	*The Hindustanee*, Vancouver, 1 Jan. 1914.

15	Statement signed by Mella, Naina Singh, Sajn Singh, Prem Singh, Pal Singh, Natha Singh, Baggat Singh, Caval Singh, Ratan Singh, Jaggatt Singh, copy, Stevens Papers.

16	Jaswant Singh 'Jas', *Baba Gurdit Singh: Komagatamaru* (Jullunder: New Book Co., 1965), p. 40. The author of this well-researched although uncritical biography in Gurmukhi had access to a handwritten account by Gurdit Singh himself. There is an account of Gurdit Singh's early life which is pure invention, in Ted Ferguson, *A White Man's Country* (Toronto: Doubleday Canada, 1975), p. 13.

17	Memo on Hindu migration, 22 Jan. 1914, US Immigration 52903/110; Burjor to Hopkinson, 30 Jan. 1914.

18	Daniel J. Keefe to A. Warner Parker, 7 Dec. 1913, US Immigration 52903/110.

19	Malcolm Reid to H. W. Brodie, C.P.R. General Passenger Agent, 20 Sept. 1913, Immigration 536999(PEI RO).

CHAPTER 3: DEPARTURE

1 Jaswant Singh 'Jas', *Baba Gurdit Singh*, pp. 9–24.
2 Ibid., p. 42.
3 Lt. Col. D. C. Phillott, Short precis of Dr Rughunath Singh's report, 6 Aug. 1914, copy, C.O. 42/985.
4 Borden to W. J. Roche, Minister of the Interior, 3 June 1914, copy, Borden Papers.
5 This is one of the points at issue—just how well Gurdit Singh understood the Canadian law. In a Panjabi language advertisement published on 13 Feb. he wrote: 'Had we any ship of our own we would have taken advantage of that period during which the Immigration laws were cancelled, and we would have been able to land numbers of our own brethren.' This is part of an extract sent from the intelligence office in Simla to J. A. Wallinger in London, 27 April 1914: C.O. 42/979. There is a reference in the *Report of the Komagata Maru Committee of Inquiry* (Calcutta, 1914), p. 2.
6 Criminal Intelligence Office, Simla, to Wallinger, 27 April 1914.
7 Jaswant Singh, *Baba Gurdit Singh*, p. 45. *Lloyd's Register* for 1913–14 shows the *Hong Bee*, 3229 tons and built in 1876 and the *Hong Moh*, 3910 tons and built in 1881. They were owned by Lim Peng Siang of Singapore.
8 Copy of the charter contract, Immigration 879545(3).
9 Jaswant Singh, *Baba Gurdit Singh*, pp. 48–9; Baba Gurdit Singh, *Voyage of Komagatamaru: or India's Slavery Abroad* (Calcutta, n.d), pt. 1, pp. 36–7.
10 Interview, 25 Sept. 1976, with Kartar Singh of the village of Mehli, Jullundur, who was a passenger on the *Komagata Maru*, and who landed at Vancouver airport on 14 Sept. 1976, for his first visit to Canada after his unsuccessful attempt to gain entry in 1914.
11 Severn described the meeting in a 300-word memo enclosed in Governor May's despatch to the Colonial Secretary, 8 April 1914 (copy to the Governor-General of Canada, Governor-General's Numbered Files 332 B, Public Archives Canada). We also have Gurdit Singh's version, a complete dialogue that appears on pp. 38–43 of pt. 1 of his *Voyage of Komagatamaru*. According to Gurdit Singh, Severn agreed to help by writing to the Canadian and Indian governments. 'Would you, if necessary, employ the same principles of passive resistance which Mr Gandhi nowadays employs in South Africa?' Severn is supposed to have asked. 'Oh yes, certainly in the like manner...' is Gurdit Singh's purported reply. But this is not consistent with Gurdit Singh's style or actions in 1914 and seems to have been added when he prepared his account for publication during Gandhi's *satyagraha* campaign in 1920-1. In other respects, the dialogue tallies so well with Severn's memo that one must conclude it is based on notes made soon after the conversation.
12 Governor May to Colonial Secretary, 8 April 1914, enclosure no. 1.

13 Borden to W. J. Roche, Minister of the Interior, Borden to Joseph Pope, Under-Secretary of State for External Affairs, and Borden to J. F. Crowly, Governor-General's Office, 7 April 1914, Borden Papers.

14 Extract from *China Press*, Shanghai, 12 April 1914, C.O. 42/979.

15 Ibid.

16 Translation of letter from Nanak Singh to Duleep Singh, 9 April 1914, Governor-General's Numbered Files 332 B.

17 H. Paske Smith, British Consulate, Simonoseki, to Sir W. Conygham Green, British Embassy, Tokyo, 2 May 1914, Governor-General's Numbered Files 332 B.

18 Jaswant Singh, pp. 57–8. He draws on a diary kept by Gurdit Singh. Evidence of venereal infections attributed to the stop at Moji was discovered during the medical examination in Vancouver: Reid to Scott, 25 June 1914, copy, Stevens Papers.

19 Phillott, Precis of Dr Rughunath Singh's report; substance of an article in *Osaka Mainichi*, Osaka, Japan, 21 April 1914, Governor-General's Numbered Files 332 B.

20 Second Supplementary Lahore Conspiracy Case, Judgment, 4 Jan. 1917, Individual case of Balwant Singh, accused no. 3, pp. 56–67; Sir Michael O'Dwyer, *India as I Knew It* (London: Constable, 1926), p. 196.

21 Reid to Scott, 26 May 1914, enclosures, Immigration 879545(1).

22 *Report of Komagata Maru Committee*, appendix iv.

23 Kartar Singh, who was among the fourteen who boarded at Yokohama, said, when interviewed on 25 Sept. 1976, that the cabins were given to Gurdit Singh and the members of the Passengers Committee. The number of cabin passengers is given in Scott to Dr G. L. Milne, Immigration Agent, Victoria, 7 May 1914, Immigration 879545(1).

24 Jaswant Singh, p. 61.

CHAPTER 4: ARRIVAL

1 H. L. Good to Malcolm Reid, 24 May 1914, and Reid to Scott, 23 May 1914, Immigration 879545(1).

2 Hopkinson to Cory, 27 May 1914, copy, Governnor-General's Numbered Files 332 B; B. A. McKelvie, *Magic, Murder and Mystery* (Duncan, B. C.: Cowichan Leader, 1966), p. 42. McKelvie of the *Daily Province* tagged along with the officials.

3 In filling out his personal data sheet for the Department of the Interior, Hopkinson gave his place and date of birth as Hull, Yorkshire, England, 16 June 1880, although he was born in Delhi as the baptismal records of the India Office show. His parents were William and Agnes Hopkinson, then residing in Allahabad, but Agnes may have been the European name of an Indian wife. The obituaries that appeared after his death say, incorrectly, that he was brought out to India as a child. They also add four years to his age.

   Fred Taylor, who at one time shared an office with Hopkinson, told me that he was part Indian. I asked how he knew and Taylor said that you could see it by looking at him. Sharon Pollock, in her drama *The Komagata Maru Incident*, builds much on the assumption that Hopkinson was a half-caste and the worse for it.

B. A. McKelvie, who was a police reporter in 1914, tells us that Hopkinson occasionally would disguise himself as a Sikh and occupy a shack in South Vancouver where he would keep an ear to the ground for information: *Magic, Murder and Mystery*, p. 47. The story is embellished in Ferguson, *A White Man's Country*, pp. 157-9. Perhaps, when in San Francisco, Hopkinson attended Har Dayal meetings wearing a turban, but he was too well known to Sikhs in Vancouver to have maintained for long a disguise when amongst them—especially if he tried to get close to his quarry, the members of the revolutionary party. The game would have been up the moment he opened his mouth because he did not speak Panjabi well. Rahim tells us how relieved Hopkinson was when he got a chance to switch from Panjabi to Hindi: *The Hindustanee*, 1 Feb. 1914, p. 7. The Sikhs complained to the government that Hopkinson did not understand their language: petition of 130 Indians, Immigration 808722(1). Hopkinson turned to others for translation of materials written in Panjabi: Hopkinson to Cory, 9 June 1914, Governor-General's Numbered Files 332 B. When Hopkinson examined the *Komagata Maru* passengers, he put the questions in English and his assistant, Harry Gwyther, translated: Minutes of Board of Inquiry, 25 June 1914, Immigration 879545(3).

If we are to believe Gurdit Singh, Hopkinson was a corrupt official open to bribery, willing to land the passengers for £1,000 in advance and £1,000 after they were ashore. Gurdit Singh says that he would have paid, but Hopkinson wanted him to swear on the *Guru Granth Sahib* never to mention it to anyone and this Gurdit Singh says he would not do: Gurdit Singh, *Komagatamaru*, pt. 1, pp. 50–1. The story does not ring true because Hopkinson did not have it in his power to do so. There was too much public and official attention focused on the ship. However, it was a good line for Gurdit Singh to give the passengers to keep them behind him. I draw this conclusion even though Kartar Singh, when interviewed on 25 Sept. 1976, and again on 22 June 1977, told me that he had heard Hopkinson say that he would get them all off for 6,000 rupees. Kartar Singh also said that Hopkinson took a pound each from the twenty men who were landed. But it was Hopkinson's job to go on board to ask each passenger to show his money and to explain that those with less than $200 could not be landed under Canadian law. It would have been easy enough for Gurdit Singh and his lieutenants to represent this as a demand for a bribe.

4 Hopkinson to Cory, 27 May 1914; *Daily Province*, 22 May 1914; *The Daily News-Advertiser*, Vancouver, 23 May 1914.
5 Reid to Scott, 26 May 1914, Immigration 879545(1).
6 Gurdit Singh to Reid, 23 May 1914, reproduced in Gurdit Singh,

Voyage of Komagatamaru, pt. 1, pp. 58–9. When Gurdit Singh assembled the material for his history, he wrote to the law firm in Vancouver that had handled his case, MacNeil, Bird, Macdonald, and Darling, and they sent him copies of the correspondence in their files.

7 Georges Pelletier, *L'Immigration Canadienne : Les Enquêtes du Devoir* (Montreal: *Le Devoir*, 1913), pp. 12–14.

8 *Daily Province*, 27 May 1914.

9 Robie L. Reid, 'The Inside Story of the *Komagata Maru*', British *Columbia Historical Quarterly*, Jan. 1941, pp. 9–10; *Daily Province*, 28, 29 May 1914.

10 *The Hindustanee*, 1 June 1914; Hopkinson to Cory, 1 June 1914, copy, C.O. 42/979.

11 *News-Advertiser*, 2 June 1914.

12 Scott to Mitchell, 6 June 1914, Immigration 879545(2).

13 *Daily Province*, 5 June 1914.

14 Interview with Kartar Singh. In the five months he spent aboard the *Komagata Maru*, Kartar Singh spoke to Gurdit Singh only once. He had been talking to Dr Rughunath Singh. Someone reported it so Gurdit Singh summoned him and he had to explain that there was nothing to it, that he was not conspiring. I asked Kartar Singh if he and his fellow passengers were afraid of Gurdit Singh. He said that they weren't really afraid but that Gurdit Singh did not mix with them and stayed mostly in his cabin.

Chapter 5: DELAY

1 Hopkinson to Cory, 17 June 1914, copy, Immigration 879545(2).

2 Bird to Reid, 17 June 1914, copy, Stevens Papers.

3 Reid to Scott, 19 June 1914, Immigration 879545(3).

4 Gurdit Singh, *Komagatamaru*, pt. 1, p. 65.

5 J. E. Bird to Bowser, Reid, and Walbridge, 20 June 1914, Gurdit Singh, pt. 1, pp. 66–7.

6 Statement of Babu Singh made in the presence of Reid, Hopkinson, Assistant Agent Howard, and a police detective, 18 June 1914, Immigration 879545(3).

7 Minutes of a Hindu Mass Meeting held at Dominion Hall, Vancouver, 21 June 1914, Stevens Papers.

8 Reid to Scott, 22 June 1914, citing wire from Scott of previous day, Immigration 879545(3).

9 Reid to Stevens, 30 June 1914, Stevens Papers.

10 Transcript of conversation between Stevens and Dr Rughunath Singh, Stevens Papers. The transcript is dated Saturday, 18 June 1914, but Saturday was the 20th.

11 Borden received telegrams from the provincial premier, Sir Richard McBride, the City of New Westminster, the Richmond Central Con-

servative Association, and the Mayor of Vancouver, all dated 23 June; Borden Papers.

12 *Daily Province*, 24 June 1914.
13 Ibid., 23 June 1914.
14 Robertson to Cory, 25 June 1914, Immigration 879545 (2).
15 *Daily Province*, 25 June 1914.

CHAPTER 6: THE COURT OF APPEAL

1 Minutes of a Board of Inquiry held in the Dominion Immigration Office, C.P.R. Wharf, Vancouver, 25 June 1914, Immigration 879545 (3).
2 This is Gurdit Singh's account, *Komagatamaru*, pt. 2, p. 7: 'Quite against the wish of the passengers, the port authorities selected one person named Munshi Singh whom the Canadian C.I.D. knew to be the fittest person for its own purpose and submitted his case before the court.'
3 Reid to Scott, 26 June 1914, Stevens Papers; Gurdit Singh, pt. 1, pp. 72–5.
4 Extract from confidential weekly diary, Superintendent of Police, Lahore, week ending 13 June 1914; Chief Commissioner, Delhi Province to Secretary, Govt of India, Commerce and Industry, 8 July 1914; Financial Secretary, Panjab Government, to Secretary, Govt of India, Commerce and Industry, 18 Aug. 1914, copies, C.O. 42/985.
5 Reid to Scott, 25 June 1914, Immigration 879545 (3).
6 Transcript, Court of Appeal proceedings at Victoria, 29 and 30 June 1914, copy, C.O. 42/980.
7 Hopkinson to Reid, 3 July 1914, copy, Stevens Papers.
8 Gurdit Singh to Bird, 5 July 1914, Gurdit Singh, *Komagatamaru*, pt. 1, pp. 76–8. He claimed he acted under compulsion: 'Now our other passengers threaten me that if I allow the men to come on board they will certainly kill me.' But he clearly acted in his own interest here and was in complete command of the ship. I asked Kartar Singh how the Passengers Committee was chosen, wondering if they represented a challenge to Gurdit Singh. 'Baba had faith in these five people', he said. 'That is why they were kept.'
9 Conversation between Mr Reid and Captain Yamamoto, 4 July 1914, copy, Stevens Papers.
10 Reid to Scott, 7 July 1914, copy, Stevens Papers.
11 Interview between Mr C. Gardner Johnson, Mr Reid, and Captain Yamamoto, copy, Stevens Papers.
12 *The Sun*, Vancouver, 7 July 1914.

CHAPTER 7: FORCE

1 Reid to Scott, 8 July 1914, copy, Stevens Papers.
2 *Daily Province*, 8 July 1914.

3   Conversation on Powell St., copy, Stevens Papers; Reid to Scott, 11 July 1914, Immigration 879545(4).
4   Statement by Bela Singh, 18 June 1914, Immigration 879545(3).
5   Scott to C. J. Doherty, Acting Minister of the Interior, 8 July 1914, copy, Immigration 879545(3).
6   Meeting of the Committee Appointed by the Passengers, 9 July 1914, copy, Stevens Papers; Passengers to editor of *News-Advertiser*, 10 July 1914, copy, Immigration 879545(4).
7   Reid to Scott, 11 July 1914, Immigration 879545(4); Hopkinson to Cory, 10 July 1914, copy, C.O. 42/980; *Daily Province, Sun, News-Advertiser, Daily World*, 10 July 1914. Reid said enough afterwards to indicate he had been in real danger. Headlines read: 'Hindus try to hold Mr Reid as Hostage'. But Hopkinson, in a full report, while describing the situation as serious and potentially explosive, did not mention any threat to Reid. The passengers wrote the *News-Advertiser*: 'Yesterday we asked Mr Reid to supply us with water and food. He replied he was thinking the matter, on this we requested him, "How long will take for consideration?" and what would be the use of that when [we] are going to starve. We set example before him, stating that if you are kept in this wretched condition for a day, you will of course come to know "What the real hunger." These are the words we spoke to Mr Reid & added, that if he will not arrange very soon, we shall be compelled to take boats to get ashore when starving. But there is a proverb "Might is right". Who hears us in our such a condition? We are at least men and feel hunger and thirst; but on requesting properly, Mr Reid says that we were going to shoot him. We never did such kind of foolish act. We request the authorities to provide us with necessities.'
8   *News-Advertiser*, 10 July 1914.
9   *Sun*, 10 July 1914.
10 Hopkinson to Cory, 10 July 1914.
11 Reid to Scott, 11 July 1914.
12 Passengers Committee to Reid, 13 July 1914, Immigration 879545(4).
13 Reid to Rughunath Singh, 11 July, Rughunath Singh to Reid, 11 and 14 July, Gurdit Singh to Reid, 12 July 1914, copies, Stevens Papers; Reid to Scott, 18 July 1914, Immigration 879545(4).
14 Hopkinson to Cory, night lettergram, 20 July 1914, copy, Governor-General's Numbered Files 332 B; Hopkinson to Samuel Backus, Commissioner of US Immigration, 20 July 1914, copy, C.O. 42/980.
15 Telephone conversation between Ladner and Hori, 18 July 1914, copy, Stevens Papers.
16 Hopkinson to Cory, 25 July 1914, copy, and Reid to Scott, same date, Immigration 879545(5).

CHAPTER 8: INTIMIDATION

1 External Affairs to Governor-General's Secretary, 4 June 1914, copy, Governor-General to Colonial Secretary, telegram, 5 June 1914, C.O. 42/979; J. D. Hazen to Borden, night lettergram, 19 July 1914, copy, Governor-General's Numbered Files 332 B.
2 Borden to G. H. Perley, 17 July 1914, Borden Papers.
3 Passengers to Balwant Singh 19 July 1914, copy, Stevens Papers.
4 Gurdit Singh, *Komagatamaru*, pt. 1, p. 108; *World*, 21 July 1914; interview with Kartar Singh, 22 June 1977. Gurdit Singh says that some of his countrymen on shore signalled that they would set fire to the whole of Vancouver, if the *Komagata Maru* men were sacrificed, and that when the officials found out, they changed their tune and began to negotiate. It would be a better story if one could believe that such an extensive fire could be started or if there was some evidence that the officials were aware of the plan.
5 Reid to Scott, 20 July 1914, Immigration 879545 (4).
6 Burrell to Borden, 25 July 1914, Borden Papers.
7 Robie Reid, *B. C. Historical Quarterly*, Jan. 1941, p. 20.
8 Copies of this telegram and two others were obtained from the Great Northwestern Telegraph Co. by the Justice Dept. on request from the Immigration Branch: letter from Justice Dept., 14 Oct. 1914, Immigration 879545 (6).
9 Burrell to Borden, 25 July 1914, Borden Papers.
10 MacNeill to Borden, 22 July 1914, Borden Papers.
11 Viceroy to Secretary of State for India, private telegram, 20 July 1914, C.O. 42/984; Colonial Secretary to Governor-General, paraphrase of cypher telegram, 20 July 1914, Borden Papers; Governor-General to Colonial Secretary, 22 July 1914, Governor-General's Numbered Files 332 B.
12 Hopkinson to Cory, 25 July 1914.
13 Ibid.
14 Reid to Scott, 25 July 1914, immigration 879545 (5).
15 Reid to Scott, 25 July 1914; Interview with Kartar Singh, 25 Sept. 1976.
16 Robertson to Cory, memorandum, 29 July 1914, Asiatic Immigration (Confidential Prints); Governor of Hong Kong to Governor-General, telegram, 23 July 1914, copy, Borden Papers.
17 Stevens to Borden, 29 July 1914, enclosing letters from J. S. Henderson, British Columbian Field Secretary, the Presbyterian Church of Canada Board of Social Service and Evangelism, S. D. Chown, General Superintendent, The Methodist Church of Canada, and R. J. Wilson, minister, St. Andrews Church, Vancouver: Borden Papers.

CHAPTER 9: RETURN

1 Interview with Kartar Singh, 25 Sept. 1976; Jaswant Singh, p. 90,
   citing Sohan Singh whom he interviewed on 30 Dec. 1964; G. S. Deol,
   The Role of the Ghadar Party in the National Movement (Delhi:
   Sterling, 1969), p. 93, citing Bhagwan Singh interviewed on 18 March
   1961; summary of evidence from the passengers of the *Komagata
   Maru* enclosed in Wheeler to Holderness, 10 Feb. 1915, copy, Immigration 879545(6); Lahore Conspiracy Case, Judgment, 13 Sept. 1915,
   Individual case of Sohan Singh, accused no. 74.
2 Gurdit Singh, *Komagatamaru*, pt. 2, p. 26.
3 Lahore Conspiracy Case, A(2) Preparing for the Migration, p. 1.
4 Interview with Kartar Singh, 22 June 1977; *Report of Komagata Maru
   Committee*, pp. 12–14.
5 Gurdit Singh, *Komagatamaru*, pt. 2, p. 29. He says they had obtained
   £7,000 from their friends in Canada and elsewhere. I questioned Kartar
   Singh on this, and, while he was not in the group close to Gurdit
   Singh, he was aware that well over £1,000 had been sent to the
   Komagata Maru in Japan. *The Bengalee*, 4 Oct. 1914, carried a *Japan
   Herald* interview with Jawahar Mal.
6 *Proceedings of the Council of the Governor-General of India*, vol. 59,
   1914–15, pp. 5–6.
7 Governor-General to Colonial Secretary, telegram, 31 Aug. 1914, Asiatic
   Immigration, Borden Papers; *Report of Komagata Maru Committee*,
   pp. 14–15.
8 Gurdit Singh, *Komagatamaru*, pt. 2, pp. 29–30.
9 *The Pioneer Mail*, Allahabad, 2 Oct. 1914.
10 O'Dwyer, *India as I Knew It*, p. 193; *Report of the Komagata Maru
   Committee*, p. 14.
11 Gurdit Singh, *Komagatamaru*, pt. 2, pp. 31–4; *Report of Komagata
   Maru Committee*, p. 23. Gurdit Singh never did admit that his people
   were armed at Budge Budge.
12 Sir Frederick Halliday's testimony at coroner's inquest, *The Bengalee*,
   13 Oct. 1914, and *The Pioneer Mail*, 16 Oct. 1914. This fits in reason-
   ably well with Gurdit Singh's graphic account of the interview: pt. 2,
   pp. 35–9.
13 Gurdit Singh says that after he and his committee had been left to
   consult for half an hour, a European officer came up to them, watch
   in hand, saying 'Get down, be quick or you will be killed. I give you
   fifteen minutes.' With ten minutes to go there was the same warning;
   at five, again, it was shouted out for all to hear. Then the steamer's
   siren blew, and the officer shouted that if they did not get off they
   would be taken out to sea and shot.
      Who is to say now that one or two police officers did not use such
   tactics? However, it is clear from Halliday's testimony that the police
   did not have the power to force the passengers to do anything if they
   chose to resist. I asked Kartar Singh, who was there, why he got down

off the ship, and he said that the officials promised that all their losses would be repaid if they got off. He mentioned no threats.

14 Gurdit Singh, *Komagatamaru*, pt. 2, pp. 41–5; *Report of the Komagata Maru Committee*, p. 15; Halliday's testimony, *The Bengalee*, 13 Oct. 1914.

15 Halliday's testimony. When the main body of passengers started for Calcutta, Kartar Singh was one of those who hung back. He had been a trooper; he knew Deputy Commissioner Humphreys, and spoke to him. Humphreys told him that there would be trouble and that he should go after the people from his own district, Jullundur, to advise them to come back. He tried to persuade them to do so, but they said he should come with them, so he returned to the Commissioner and said he had not been able to talk to anyone, shrugging off the responsibility. Then he got on the train: interview, 25 Sept. 1976.

16 The exchange is taken verbatim from Gurdit Singh, *Komagatamaru*, pt. 2, pp. 45–6. One can trust neither the official account nor Gurdit Singh except when one confirms the other. In this case, it is clear from a Bengal Government statement published in *The Bengalee*, 2 Oct. 1914, that such an exchange did take place.

17 Who fired the first shot? Gurdit Singh says the passengers were unarmed, but there is too much evidence to the contrary. Yet one cannot rely on the findings of the official inquiry which blamed the passengers. Among those involved in the riot, there were probably few who saw how it started and fewer who saw and testified truthfully. Sohan Singh Josh, in his book, *Tragedy of Komagata Maru* (New Delhi: People's Publishing House, 1975), pp. 77, 108, quotes Harnam Singh Gujarwal, one of Gurdit Singh's inner circle, who said that Eastwood fired twice after his *lathi* was grabbed from him. He hit Thakur Singh and sent a bullet through Harnam Singh's headgear. 'Munsha Singh snatched a pistol from him and killed him then and there.' However, Bishen Singh of Chuharchak village, Ferozepore, who sailed on the *Komagata Maru* at the age of fifteen or sixteen, and who was wounded in the right arm during the riot, told Sohan Singh that Bhan Singh of Mundapind, Amritsar, fired the first shot, killing Eastwood. There was no Bhan Singh of Mundapind listed among the passengers at Budge Budge, but confusion in names after sixty years is excusable. There was a Keshu Singh, alias Sher Singh, alias Buttan Singh of Mundapind.

CHAPTER 10: ARREST AND DETENTION

1 *The Bengalee*, 3 Oct. 1914; *Report of Komagata Maru Committee*, p. 18.
2 Gurdit Singh, *Komagatamaru*, pt. 2, pp. 52–60.
3 *The Bengalee*, 3 Oct. 1914.
4 Ibid., 2 Oct. 1914.
5 Ibid., 3 Oct. 1914.

6 25 Sept. 1976 interview with Kartar Singh who was on the train.

7 *The Pioneer Mail*, 9 Oct. 1914; *The Bengalee*, 4, 6 and 7 Oct. 1914; *Report of the Komagata Maru Committee*, pp. 29–30 and appendix iv.

8 *The Pioneer Mail*, 9 and 16 Oct. 1914.

9 6 Oct. 1914.

10 *The Bengalee*, 14 Oct 1914.

11 17 Oct. 1914.

12 Gurdit Singh, *Komagatamaru*, pt. 2, pp. 89–90; *Report of Komagata Maru Committee*, appendix iv, p. 9. Gurdit Singh says there was a reward of 2,000 rupees for his arrest. However, it was published as 1,000 rupees in *The Pioneer Mail*, 16 Oct. 1914.

13 Summary of evidence bearing on the supply of pistols to the passengers of the *Komagata Maru*, enclosed in Wheeler to Holderness, 10 Feb. 1915, copy, Immigration 879545 (6).

14 Ibid.

15 *The Pioneer Mail*, 11 Dec. 1914.

16 Summary of evidence bearing on the supply of pistols.

17 *Report of Komagata Maru Committee*, p. 47; *Supplement to the Gazette of India*, 16 Jan. 1915, Resolution dated 13 Jan. 1915, paragraph 5.

18 Gurdit Singh, *Komagatamaru*, pt. 2, pp. 90–2. A *Ghadr* party booklet, *The Second Echo of the Ghadr*, with an account of the *Komagata Maru* by Bhagwan Singh Jakh was translated for the Immigration Dept. by Bela Singh: copy, Stevens Papers.

19 Lahore Conspiracy Case, Judgment, 13 Sept. 1915, A(3) The objects of going to India, p. 2.

20 *The Pioneer Mail*, 6 Nov 1914.

21 Deol, *The Ghadar Party in the National Movement*, pp. 108–48.

22 Ibid., pp. 141–3.

23 Lahore Conspiracy Case, Judgment, 13 Sept. 1915, Individual cases of Bishen Singh, accused no. 10, and Gurmukh Singh, accused no. 17. Gurmukh Singh was kept in the Andaman Islands prison from Dec. 1915 until July 1921 and led several hunger strikes against the prison authorities. He escaped from a moving train when he was brought back to India to be transferred to an Indian prison in 1921. After some years in Afghanistan and the Soviet Union, he returned to India where he worked underground until he was arrested in 1936. He was still in prison in Lahore in Dec. 1945: Randir Singh, *The Ghadar Heroes: Forgotten Story of the Punjab Revolutionaries of 1914* (Bombay: People's Publishing House, 1945), pp. 27–8, 30, and 33.

24 This was the experience of Kartar Singh as he described it on 25 Sept. 1976. In April 1917, the Lieutenant-Governor of the Panjab announced that he still had over 1,000 men restricted to their villages in addition to the 154 returned emigrants in jail: Ker, pp. 363–4.

25 They were Balwant Singh, Battan Singh, Kartar Singh, and Munsha Singh, accused no. 3, 4, 11, and 13: Second Supplementary Lahore Conspiracy Case, Judgment 4 Jan. 1917, pp. 56–70, and 76–83. Balwant

Singh was the only one hanged; the others were transported for life. Some of the *Ghadr*ites were released at the end of the war, but others served for twenty years.

CHAPTER 11: SURRENDER

1 Gurdit Singh, *Komagatamaru*, pt. 2, pp. 97–125.
2 *Young India*, 17 Nov. 1921.
3 K. M. Panikkar and A. Pershad (eds.), *The Voice of Freedom: Selected Speeches of Pandit Motilal Nehru* (Bombay, 1961), p. 9.
4 Gurdit Singh, *Komagatamaru*, pt. 2, pp. 129–31. Gandhi appeared in the High Court, Bombay, on 3 March and spoke at a public meeting in Bombay on 5 March. He was back at his *ashram* in Ahmedabad, 10, 11, 13, and 14 March and in Bombay 16, 17, 18, and 19 March. This is given in the correspondence and chronology in *The Collected Works of Mahatma Gandhi* (Government of India, 1965).
5 Gurdit Singh, *Komagatamaru*, pt. 2, pp. 143–4.
6 Khushwant Singh, *A History of the Sikhs* (Princeton University Press, 1966), vol. 2, pp. 198–200; Ruchi Ram Singh, *Struggle for Reform in Sikh Temples* (Amritsar, n. d.), pp. 62 ff.
7 Speech at Punjab Sabha Meeting, Calcutta, 7 Sept. 1921, *The Collected Works of Mahatma Gandhi*, vol. 21, pp. 61–2.
8 Gurdit Singh, *Komagatamaru*, pt. 2, p. 147–8; 'Special Session of Sikh Central League, Amritsar, 24 June 1923', H. N. Mitra (ed.), *The Indian Annual Register, 1923*, pp. 967–8; also *The Indian Annual Register, 1922*, p. 53.
9 1 Dec. 1921.
10 Jaswant Singh, *Baba Gurdit Singh*, pp. 207–9.
11 Ramsharan Vidyarthi, *Komagata Maru ki Sumudri Yatra* (Mirajpur: Krantikara Publications, 1970), pp. 98–9.
12 Bose, *Indian Revolutionaries Abroad*, pp. 62–3 n.

CHAPTER 12: ASSASSINATION

1 Hopkinson to Cory, 11 Aug. 1914, copy, Immigration 536999(1); A. T. Skak to Hopkinson, 19 Aug. 1914, Immigration 536999(PEI RO).
2 Reid to Scott, 20 Aug. 1914, and G. L. Milne, Immigration Agent, Victoria, to Scott, 27 Aug. 1914, Immigration 536999(PEI RO).
3 *Daily Province*, 1 Sept. 1914.
4 Ibid., 4 Sept. and 10 Nov. 1914; *News-Advertiser*, 6 Nov. 1914; *Sun*, 6 Nov. 1914.
5 *Sun*, 5 Nov. 1914; McKelvie, pp. 48–9.
6 *News-Advertiser*, 6 and 8 Sept. and 6 Nov. 1914; *Sun*, 5, 6, 18, and 21 Nov. 1914.
7 Statement by Mella *et al.*, Dec. 1913 and conversation on Powell St.,

11

8 July 1914, copies, Stevens Papers; statement by Bela Singh, 18 June 1914, copy, Immigration 879545(3).

8 Evidence of witnesses Polley, Cadwell, Campbell, and McCann reported in the *World*, 24 and 30 Oct.; Reid to Scott, 22 Oct. 1914, Immigration 808722(2).

9 *Sun*, 26 Oct. 1914.

10 Harcourt to Arthur, 25 Sept. 1914 and telegram, 28 Oct. 1914, and Reid to Cory, 31 Oct. 1914, Asiatic Immigration, Borden Papers; Scott and Robertson to Roche, 3 Dec. 1914, Robertson to Nellie Hopkinson, 21 July 1915, and Scott to Cory, 27 Aug. 1918, Immigration 808722(2); interview with Fred Taylor, 29 Oct. 1976.

11 Scott to Cory, 7 Nov. 1914, Immigration 536999(1). This was in response to a telegram from Harcourt to Arthur, 4 Nov. 1914.

12 Scott and Robertson to Cory, 3 Dec. 1914. Reid told his friends that Robertson was against him because 'I had sat tight on the Oriental Question': Reid to Stevens, 29 Feb. 1916, Stevens Papers. Fred Taylor, when interviewed, said that Reid was removed because he was unreliable and on poor terms with his staff. If the *Komagata Maru* had not focused attention on him, he might have lasted longer.

13 Reid to Scott, 22 Oct. 1914, Immigration 808722(2).

14 This was what Hopkinson feared: Hopkinson to Cory, night lettergram, 20 July 1914.

15 Reid to Scott, 8 Aug. 1915, copy, Borden Papers; statement of Mewa Singh, copy, Stevens Papers; Robertson to Doherty, 4 Jan. 1915, Immigration 808722(2).

16 Gurdit Singh, drawing on *Ghadr* sources, tells Mewa Singh's story this way: pt. 2, pp. 17–20.

17 *Sun*, 31 Oct 1914.

18 In charging the second jury, Judge Aulay Morrison said that instead of pursuing the prisoner, it should have been the duty of the crown to protect him: *Sun*, 18 Nov. 1914.

19 Reid to Scott, telegram, 5 Dec. 1914, Immigration 808722(2).

20 Second Supplementary Lahore Conspiracy Case, Individual cases of Balwant Singh and Kartar Singh, pp. 56–67 and 76–80.

21 *News-Advertiser*, 14 April 1915.

22 Report of H. C. Clogstoun, Nov. 1915, pp. 8–9, copy, Borden Papers; Reid to Scott, 10 Aug. 1915, Immigration 536999(9).

23 Jaswant Singh, *Baba Gurdit Singh*, p. 88 n.; Second Supplementary Lahore Conspiracy Case, II(4) The Revolutionary Movement in Canada, pp. 35–6.

24 Report of H. C. Clogstoun, 5 Nov. 1914, pp. 27–8, copy, Borden Papers; Burrell to Roche, 24 Oct. 1916, Immigration 879545(7).

25 Note on the Hindu Revolutionary Movement in Canada [March 1919], pp. 12–13, Immigration 536999(11).

26 Kalyan Kumar Banerjee, 'The U.S.A. and Indian Revolutionary Activity: Early Phase of the *Gadar* Movement', *Modern Review*, Feb. 1965, pp. 99–100. This is more sophisticated than Giles T. Brown, 'The

Hindu Conspiracy, 1914–17', *Pacific Historical Quarterly*, Aug. 1948, pp. 307–8.

27 J. S. Bains, 'The Ghadr Movement: A Golden Chapter in Indian Nationalism', *Indian Journal of Political Science*, Jan./March 1962, pp. 53–6.

28 Pope to Borden, memorandum, 22 Jan. 1916, Borden Papers; Scott to Pope, 7 Jan. 1916, Immigration 536999(9); India Office confidential memorandum, Dept. of External Affairs, *Documents on Canadian External Affairs*, vol. I (Ottawa, 1967), p. 666.

29 O. D. Skelton, External Affairs, to F. C. Blair, Immigration, 9 Sept. 1939, Immigration 536999(16): 'I need not remind you that the *Komagata Maru* incident coincided pretty closely with the outbreak of the last Great War, and that its repercussions in India proved to be profound and disturbing. I think that, on grounds of general policy, we should do everything we can to prevent the recurrence of anything that might be remotely compared to that unfortunate affair.'

30 Khalsa Diwan Society, *Report on Dominion, Provincial, and Municipal Franchise for Hindus in British Columbia* (Victoria, 1947), pp. 5–9; Gray R. Hess, 'The "Hindu" in America: Immigration and Naturalization Policies and India, 1917–1956', *Pacific Historical Review*, 1969, pp. 71–7.

INDEX

Moore, Captain Francis, 102, 103, 104
Mukerjee, Jatindranath, 124
Munsha Singh Takhan of Jundiala, 22
Munsha Singh, passenger, 149
Munshi Singh, passenger, 52, 54–6, 57, 58, 59, 60, 61
Murphy, Justice Denis, 18, 19
Muslims, on *Komagata Maru,* 33, 36, 98
Mutiny of 1857, 7, 25

Nabha, Maharaja of, 56
Nagata, Akira, 31, 92
Nagpur Congress, 119–20
Nanak Chand, Sub-Inspector, 102
Nanak Singh of Rawalpindi, passenger, 30
Nankana: massacre, 120; festival, 121–2
Narain Das, 93, 95, 96, 111
Narain Singh, passenger, 52
Native Indians of Canada, 60
The News-Advertiser, Vancouver, 70–1, 76
Nehru, Jawaharlal, 119, 124
Nehru, Motilal, 117, 118, 119
Niagara, S.S., 84
Niobe, Canadian cruiser, 79

O'Dwyer, Sir Michael, Governor of the Panjab, 33, 114, 117
Osaka Shosen Kaisha, 23, 33

Panama Maru, S.S., 17–18, 20, 39
Pandia, Dr D. P., 135–6
Panjab, Government of, 96, 105, 122
    Governor of, Sir Michael O'Dwyer, 33, 114, 117
    Assembly, 123
24-Parganas, Magistrate of, James Donald, 97, 99–100, 102, 110
Partap Singh Kairon, politician, 123
Passengers Committee, 25, 26, 29–30, 69, 142, 144, 145
Patiala, Maharaja of, 56

Patel, V. J., Congress leader of Gujarat, 118
Patrol boats, 36, 38–9, 50
Petrie, David, Panjab Police Officer, 102
Pir Baksh of Nurenahal, passenger, 110
Pohlo Ram of Anandpur, passenger, 46, 56, 106, 110
Polley, Richard, court employee, 128
Pratt, Frank D., law student, 68
Provincial Assembly of British Columbia, 6
The Province, Vancouver, 22, 30, 51, 66

Rahim, Husain (Chagan Kairaj Varma), 52, 55, 62; leadership role, 9, 40–1, 48–9; arrival in Canada, 9; and self-government, 9–10, 136; and explosives, 9, 10, 67, 139; and Hopkinson, 9, 37, 143; and Sikhs, 11–12; and Bird, 18, 39, 56; and murderous talk, 22, 67, 126, 127–8; attempted interception of *Komagata Maru,* 35–6; and test case, 40; and food and water, 43, 56; and charter, 45, 47–8; and negotiations, 65–6, 71–2, 73, 76, 81, 83, 85; on board *Komagata Maru,* 87–8, 93–4; arrested, 132; and Shore Committee funds, 133
Rainbow, Canadian cruiser, 79–81
Rajah Singh, 35, 49
Reid, Malcolm R. J.: appointment 19, 140; and Stevens, 19, 50; and Bhagwan Singh, 19–20; and the courts, 19–20, 47, 49–50, 52–3; and threats, 26, 67, 68, 115, 127–8; advised of *Komagata Maru,* 30–1; meets ship, 35, 36–7; strategy, 38–44, 45, 47–8, 68; and food and water, 42–3, 56, 70, 71, 88; and use of force, 46, 52, 57, 62–4, 71, 72, 73, 74–7, 81–3, 88–9; and Munshi Singh, 52–3, 54;